Sailing for Everyone

by

Simon Watts

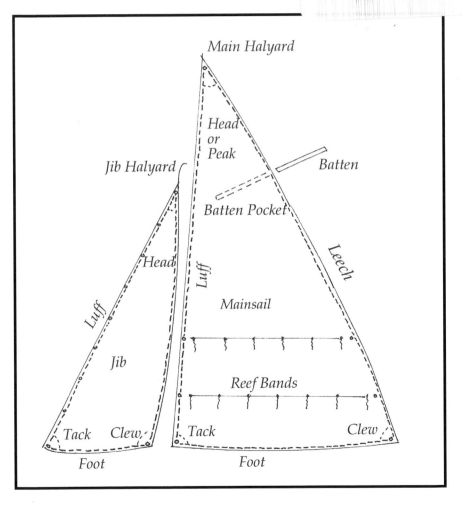

Main Halyard

Head or Peak

Batten

Jib Halyard

Batten Pocket

Leech

Head

Luff

Luff

Mainsail

Jib

Reef Bands

Tack Clew

Tack

Clew

Foot

Foot

WoodenBoat **BOOKS**
BROOKLIN, MAINE USA

Published by
WoodenBoat Books
Naskeag Road, PO Box 78
84 Great Cove Drive
Brooklin, Maine 04616 USA
www.woodenboatbooks.com

ISBN 10: 1-934982-01-6
ISBN 13: 978-1-934982-01-3

First printing 2009

Book Design: Grace Bell
Cover Design: BasRelief Design

On the front cover:
Silver Thread, a Cornish daysailer, lug sail with mizzen.
Photo by J. Karlin

All drawings by or courtesy of the author unless otherwise noted.

Printed in China by Codra Enterprises

10 9 8 7 6 5 4 3 2 1

With special thanks to

Richard, Alison, and Rebecca.

Their willingness to sail all kinds of boats

in all kinds of weather made this book possible.

Contents

Foreword

My family has owned a summer home on Middle Island, near Lunenburg, Nova Scotia, for over forty years. The children learned to sail in these chilly, fog-bound waters, and now their children are doing the same. This book is the product of the adventures and misadventures we have had over the years. It started out as a guide for family and friends but gradually evolved into a basic primer on small-boat sailing, well suited to the novice of any age.

Although written with the harsh conditions of Nova Scotia as background, wind and water are much the same the world over. You can learn to sail equally well on open sea, a river, tidal estuary, reservoir, or lake.

Years ago I taught sailing in Castine, Maine, using a locally built class of sailboat. The boat was considered very safe because it was so beamy,

"10 feet long and 9 feet wide" as people used to say. Students climbed aboard by stepping on the gunwale, (the trim along the edge) and the boat barely moved. When they tried that with my International Fourteen (a 14-foot racing boat with a 22-foot mast) the boat capsized, instantly.

I tried to explain to the students' parents that the "safe" boat was the more dangerous of the two because it encouraged bad habits, but I don't think anyone believed me. So learning to sail on some cranky, awkward boat, not too forgiving of beginners' mistakes, may well make you a better sailor in the long run.

Introduction

Obviously you need a boat, a sailboat, 10 to 16 feet in length, with two sails, a mainsail and a jib. You will have to handle a jib sooner or later, so you might as well start now. A movable keel (called a centerboard or drop keel) is preferable to a fixed one. With a centerboard you can sail on and off beaches, lakes, rivers, and other shallow water.

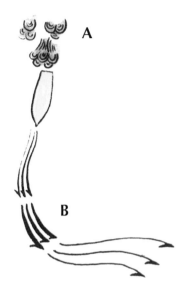

A

B

The style of boat is not important, but it should be equipped with both sails and oars. If you don't already know how to row, learn that first. Then, if you find yourself in difficulties, you can take down the sail and row home. You should also know how to swim—safer for you and less worrisome for those on shore. I remember when local fishermen were reluctant to carry life jackets. "When I go, I want to go quick—I don't want to bob around", as one said to me. Not a very sensible attitude, and one that has since changed.

Two symbols are used throughout this book, one for the wind (A) and the other for current (B). Keep in mind that a wind is known by where it's coming from (a north wind is blowing from the north), but a current by its direction of flow (a southerly current is flowing toward the south).

When I introduce an unfamiliar term for the first time, garboard, for example, I'll give a brief explanation in the text. For a more complete description, see Chapter 8, "Language of the Sea."

Chapter 1, "About the Wind," is the core of this book and explains how to handle a sailboat under different wind conditions. However, before going off on your own you need to know more than just how to sail: dealing with docks, buoys, moorings, and anchors, for example. You also need a basic understanding of the Rules of the Road—who gives way to whom and under what circumstances. You will also find several basic knots, a couple of splices, and two ways to whip the ends of a rope so it doesn't unravel.

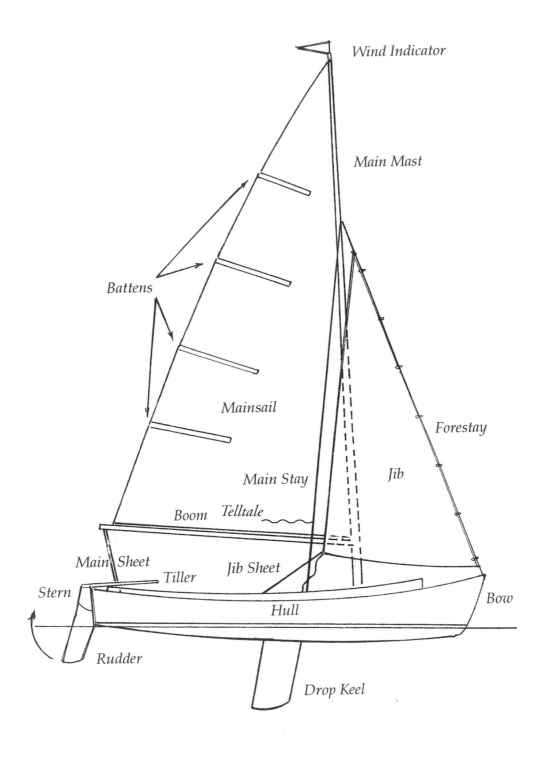

Wind Indicator

Main Mast

Battens

Mainsail

Main Stay

Forestay

Jib

Boom   Telltale

Main Sheet

Jib Sheet

Tiller

Stern

Bow

Hull

Rudder

Drop Keel

There is as yet no universal system of navigational aids—buoys, beacons, lighthouses, and fog-horns. In Chapter 6 you'll find illustrations, in color, of the basic navigation markers used in North America. There are minor differences between the Canadian and U.S. systems, but they are basically the same.

I've also included a sample chart, tide table, and where to get these useful items. Also suggestions on safety and the gear you should carry with you.

Fair-weather sailing over a sunlit sea is lovely—but it won't always be that way. It's as well to know what to do when there's too much wind, when you get lost in the fog, capsize, lose an oar, run aground, or break something. All the incidents described in Chapter 5, "When Things Go Wrong," are real ones. They've happened, and usually more than once.

At the end of Chapter 6, you will find twenty-one questions posing a variety of situations that you are likely to encounter. In each scenario you are assumed to be the skipper of a sailboat, with jib, mainsail, and oars but no engine. You have a crew of one. See if you can come up with a sensible solutions before looking up the answers at the end of the book. Remember: there are usually as many ways to get out of a jam as to get into one.

The Basic Vocabulary

Every part of a boat, even a small one, has a name. Memorize these names so you don't have to shout, "Watch out for the thingamajig!" or "Where did you put the whatsitcalled?" which is not helpful and in an emergency, downright dangerous.

Most boats, even barges, have a bow and stern as well as port and starboard sides. The only exception I can think of are coracles, which are circular. It's easy to remember which side is which because port has the same number of letters as left. Starboard, of course, is right. Port and starboard are used when facing forward, toward the bow. If you turn around and face the other way, they don't change—which is the whole point of using the correct terms.

The sketch on the opposite page shows some of the most useful names for the parts of the boat and rig—enough to get started. For a more detailed account, take a cruise through Chapter 8, "The Language of the Sea".

Happy Sailing,
Simon Watts
Nova Scotia, 2009

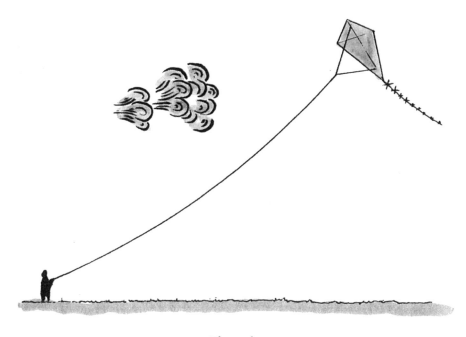

Flying kites

Chapter 1. About the Wind

*"There are three kinds of wind: too much,
too little, and right on the nose"*

—Captain Adrian Fieldhouse

The wind is the engine that powers your boat. As soon as you raise the sails, your engine is in gear—and you have no brakes. Train yourself to be constantly aware of the wind's force and direction. When the breeze is strong, there's no doubt where it's coming from. With light airs it's more difficult. Dip a finger in the water and hold it up. It feels cooler on the windward side, just as when you dry your hands with an electric blower.

It's helpful to tie a length of brightly colored yarn or wool to each stay, a foot or so above the gunwale (see page 10). These are called telltales and show the direction of the wind relative to your boat.

Before going any further, you need to know a bit about keels—both the fixed variety and drop keels, also about rudders and how they work.

Why Do Sailboats Need a Keel?

Just about everyone has flown a kite and felt the tug of the string as the kite soars higher and higher. But have you ever asked yourself what keeps a kite up? Or a flying swan or a Boeing 747? The answer, of course, is the wind blowing on an inclined surface, kite, airplane, or swan's wing. The only real difference is that kites need wind to fly but birds and planes make their own wind by flying forward through the air.

Obviously, it's the string that prevents the kite from being blown sideways. If the string breaks, or you let go, it soon comes tumbling down. So why doesn't a sailboat get blown sideways like a kite since obviously there's no string attached?

The answer is that all sailboats need some kind of vertical fin sticking down into the water. This fin is called a keel and makes it easy for the boat to go forward or backward but hard to go sideways.

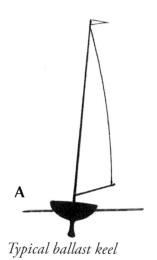

A

Typical ballast keel

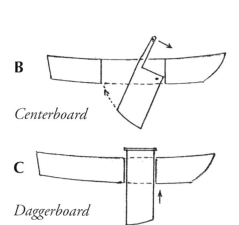

B

Centerboard

C

Daggerboard

Wind

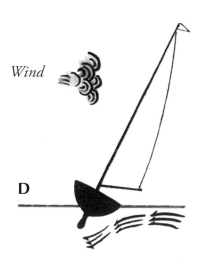

D

Different Kinds of Keel

Some keels are an integral part of the boat and are called fixed keels. They usually have iron or lead in them to help keep the boat upright; these are called ballast keels (A). Fixed keels are a nuisance because you can't easily trailer a keelboat, nor can you sail it in shallow water. Furthermore, if you run a keelboat aground you can't just jump out and push because the water is usually too deep.

For small boats—20 feet and under—an alternative to a fixed keel is the drop keel or centerboard. This is a metal or wooden plate, housed in the centerboard case or centerboard trunk (B). A centerboard is raised or lowered depending on the depth of water and the point of sailing.

A daggerboard (C) is the same idea as a centerboard, but instead of swinging up or down it slides vertically in the case. Centerboards remain in the centerboard case, whether up or down, but daggerboards have to be removed and laid in the boat, so tend to get in the way.

A further drawback to a daggerboard is that if you hit a rock, you're liable to do serious damage. Hit hard bottom with a centerboard, and it just swings up out of harm's way.

Instead of a centerboard, the old sailing barges, were fitted with a pair of swinging keels called leeboards attached to the sides of the boat. You seldom see them now, except in Holland where most of the inland water is shallow.

As you can see from the diagram (D), the further a sail boat tips, the less effective is the keel. So keep your boat as upright as possible and use the crew as movable ballast. Trim the boat by having them sit on the windward (or weather) side.

How Does a Rudder Steer?

A rudder is a hinged blade attached to the stern of the boat, usually to the transom. Pins on the rudder (called pintles) drop into sockets (gudgeons) screwed to the transom. The tiller fits into a socket at the head of the rudder and is how you actually steer. Larger boats would more likely be steered with a wheel mechanically connected to the rudder.

As you can see from the diagram (A), the rudder works by pushing the water one way, causing the bow of the boat to swing in the opposite direction. Tiller to starboard, bow to port—and vice versa. Obviously, when the water is not moving past the rudder, you can't steer at all, any more than you can steer a parked car. When there is sufficient movement to steer, it's called having steerage.

If you push the rudder too far, more than about 45 degrees, it begins to act like a brake. On the rare occasions when your boat is going backward through the water, the rudder acts in reverse—tiller to port, bow to port.

A rudder projecting below the keel is vulnerable to damage from rocks and shoal (shallow) water. Some boats are fitted with hinged blades that flip up when encountering an underwater obstruction (B).

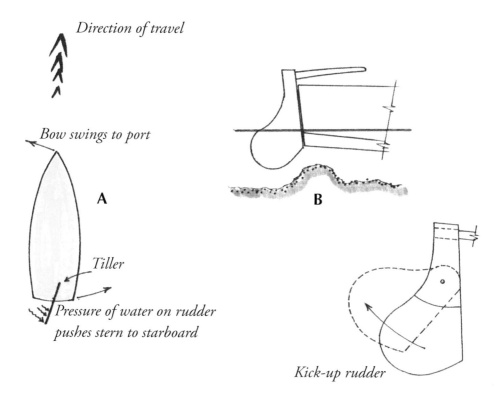

Direction of travel

Bow swings to port

A

B

Tiller

Pressure of water on rudder pushes stern to starboard

Kick-up rudder

Now, About the Wind

There are three principal points of sailing, each one defined by the direction of the wind in relation to your boat:

(A) Wind from ahead—close-hauled

(B) Wind from the side—reaching

(C) Wind from behind—running

There is actually a fourth point (D), when the wind is right on the nose, meaning directly ahead. Even the handiest boat in the world will soon start to go backward with all its sails shaking.

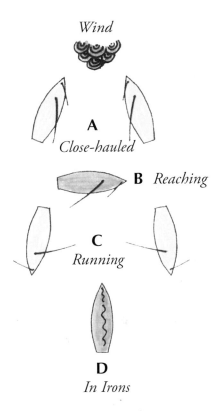

Wind from Ahead

This is also called sailing against the wind or close-hauled. Both the mainsail and jib are pulled in tight, and the centerboard should be down to minimize leeway (sideways slippage). You may also be beating to windward by a series of tacks, as explained on the next page.

Windward sailing is an exciting, often wet ride, the bow crashing into the waves, blowing the spray back onto the crew. If anything is going to break, it's liable to happen now.

You'll find there is quite a strain on the mainsheet, and it may be tiring to hold. Resist the temptation to make it fast (tie it down). If you are hit by a sudden gust of wind, you must be able to relieve the pressure on the sail by easing (letting out) the mainsheet—and quickly.

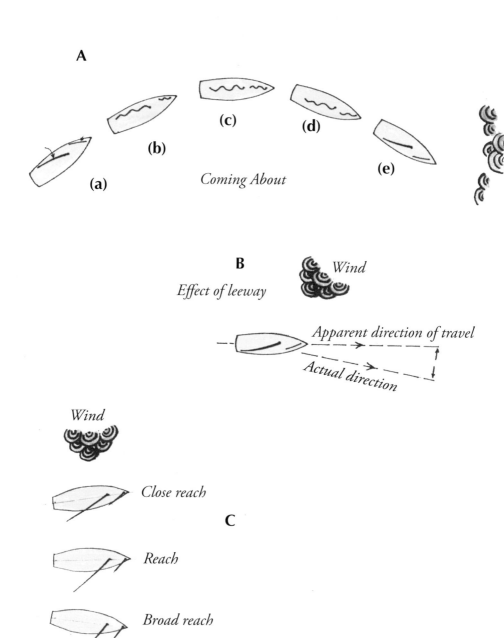

A

(c)

(d)

(b)

(a)

Coming About

(e)

B

Effect of leeway

Wind

Apparent direction of travel

Actual direction

Wind

Close reach

C

Reach

Broad reach

Tacking or Beating to Windward

Since you can't sail directly into the wind, you have to sail a zigzag course, making a series of tacks as shown in the adjacent sketch. It looks simple enough, but how do you get from one tack to the other? Changing tacks is called coming about and is shown on the opposite page (A).

Coming About

The sail is full of wind at (a); then, as you steer into the wind, the sail begins to shake (b), and is all a-tremble at (c), when the boat is pointing directly into the wind. Then it begins to settle down again (d) until you are on the opposite tack (e). Sailors call (c) being in irons (see Chapter 5).

Small, lightweight sailboats soon slow down, stop, and even go backward when pointing directly into the wind. So the trick is to get the boat moving and then go about as briskly as possible. Tell the crew what you are about to do so they can be ready to handle the jibsheets and keep their heads down. Say "Ready about" and then, when all is ready, "Lee-O", "Hard a-lee" or "Helm's a-lee" as you push the tiller over.

About Leeway

Boats sailing to windward are always slipping sideways. This slippage is called making leeway. You can reduce leeway but never eliminate it. Depending on your boat and the weather conditions, leeway can be anywhere from 15° to 30° as shown on the opposite page (B).

Wind from the Side

When sailing across the wind, you are on a reach or reaching. Both the jib and the mainsail should be about half-out and the centerboard partway down. Reaching is the easiest, most comfortable, and usually the driest point of sailing. Your little boat slides smoothly along in the trough of the waves with no fuss and little spray. If the wind is a little aft of the beam (toward the stern), you are on a broad reach; if forward (toward the bow), a close reach (C).

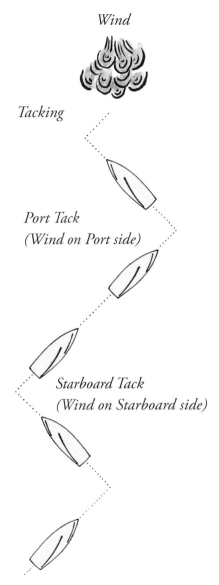

Wind

Tacking

Port Tack
(Wind on Port side)

Starboard Tack
(Wind on Starboard side)

Wind from Astern

With the wind behind, you are running or sailing downwind. Both the jib and the mainsail are all the way out. If you have a spinnaker, now is the time to hoist it.

I've left running before the wind until last because, although it looks easy, it's actually the trickiest point of sailing. For one thing, there is a greater chance of collision with another boat. This is because with both sails out in front, you can't see as well as when you are reaching or close-hauled, and so are more likely to run into another boat, buoy, or swimmer. Also, when running before the wind you can't relieve pressure on the mainsail, due to a sudden gust, by easing the mainsheet for the simple reason that the sheet is already all the way out.

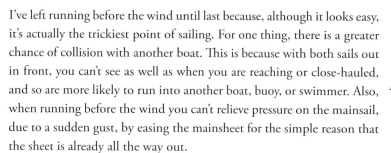

Running before the wind

When you get to Chapter 6, "Rules of the Maritime Road", you will see that a boat running before the wind must give way to those close-hauled or on a reach. This tends to limit one's options, especially in a stiff breeze because you may wish to avoid a jibe.

Jibing

Jibing is like coming about except that the wind is brought around the back of the sail, not the front. There is none of that annoying but harmless flapping as you come about. A change of course, or a puff of wind from the wrong direction will cause the boom to swing suddenly to the opposite side of the boat, and you will have jibed.

When sailing even a small boat, it's good practice to pull the mainsail in tight before jibing, as shown on the left. Then the boom doesn't swing as far, or as fast, and you are less likely to damage the boat or injure the crew. Be alert when running before the wind: keep your weight in the middle of the boat so you can shift it quickly.

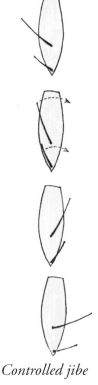

From your very first sail, get in the habit of thinking through every maneuver before carrying it out. Tell the crew what you are about to do, give them time to prepare, then do it. For example, when jibing you say "Ready to jibe" or "Standby to jibe," the crew hauls in the sheets, and positions themselves, then you say "Jibe-O" and push the tiller over. In a small sailboat this is no big deal, but if you learn to follow these routines, you will be better prepared for handling larger craft. An uncontrolled jibe can knock someone overboard as well as doing serious damage to the boat.

Controlled jibe

Broaching-To

Some sailboats, running in a strong wind with the mainsail all the way out, have a tendency to suddenly swing up into the wind. This uncontrolled turn is called broaching-to (A). It's dangerous because the boat can heel over so far that it fills with water and swamps.

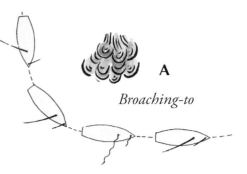

A

Broaching-to

Running by the Lee

When running before the wind you may find that the wind and the boom are on the same side of the boat as in (B). This situation is called running by the lee. It's dangerous because it's an unstable point of sailing and the boom could come swinging over with little or no warning.

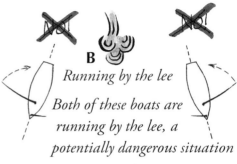

B
Running by the lee

Both of these boats are running by the lee, a potentially dangerous situation

Tacking Downwind

One way to make sure that you don't jibe accidentally is to tack downwind (C). Boat X is heading straight downwind, but boat Y is sailing at a slight angle to avoid the possibility of an accidental jibe. Eventually, when too far off course, it will make a controlled jibe and head at a slight angle the other way.

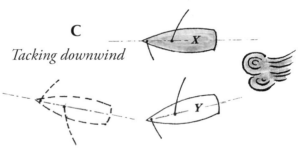

C
Tacking downwind

Bearing-up and Bearing-away

Every time you change direction, you either decrease the angle between the centerline of your boat and the wind, or you increase it (see sketch, right). The first is called bearing up, the second bearing away. It's a convenient shorthand to tell the crew what you are about to do. They can then trim the sails and position themselves accordingly.

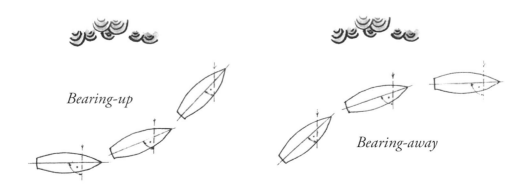

Bearing-up

Bearing-away

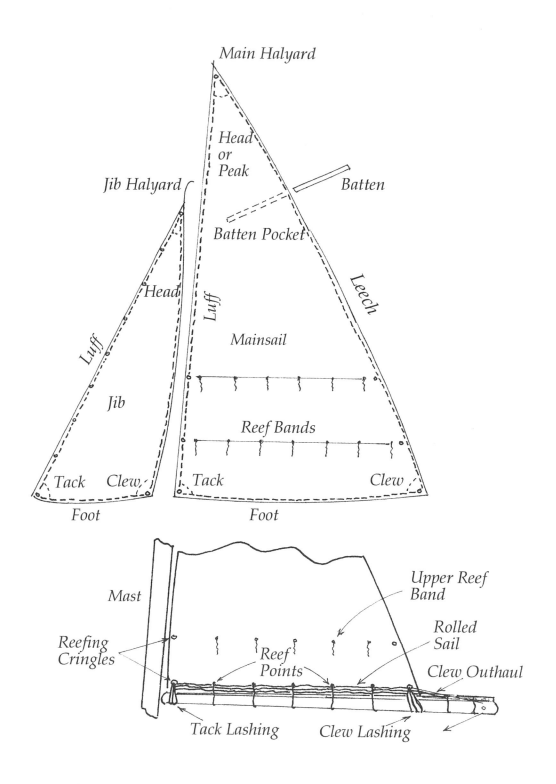

Main Halyard

Head or Peak

Batten

Jib Halyard

Batten Pocket

Head

Luff

Leech

Luff

Jib

Mainsail

Reef Bands

Tack Clew

Tack

Clew

Foot

Foot

Mast

Upper Reef Band

Reefing Cringles

Reef Points

Rolled Sail

Clew Outhaul

Tack Lashing

Clew Lashing

Chapter 2. Too Much Wind

Reefing and Other Heavy–Weather Tactics

Reefing

Reefing is a way to reduce the area of sail exposed to the wind. Small boats usually have a single or double row of reefpoints. You tie these around the boom or, if you have no boom, around the foot of the sail. If you don't have reefpoints, you should have one or more rows of grommets (brass rings sewn into the sail) through which you pass a reefing line.

Some larger boats are fitted with roller-reefing gear. Just rotate the boom, either by hand or with a crank, easing the main halyard as you wind the sail up—like a roller window blind.

The usual way to reef is to come up into the wind and lower the jib and then the mainsail. If you have crew, you might want to keep the jib up and jog along on a close reach until the mainsail is reefed and ready to be hoisted again. Roll the surplus sail into a long, tight sausage, parallel to the boom and lying tightly against it. This is awkward—but not impossible—to do alone. Tie the reefpoints around the sail using a square knot. Some people like to tuck one end in (like a shoelace), as it is easier to undo.

The opposite, called shaking out a reef, is the reverse. You may not need to lower the sail but can let go the reefpoints, then the two lashings at clew and tack, and hoist the sail back up. It's always better to reef before you need to rather than wait. If you are in doubt, look around and see what the other sailboats are doing—and not doing.

Sailing on lakes and rivers can be tricky: powerful gusts of wind may arrive with little warning, giving you no time to reef. Your best option is to let the mainsheet go, bring the boat up into the wind, and drop the sails. If the gust persists, you may need to reef or run off before the wind under jib alone, to reach shelter. See diagram (A) on the next page.

If the wind is still moderate, with only occasional strong gusts, you can often get by without reefing. Watch for the squalls (usually a dark patch moving rapidly across the surface of the water) and luff up just before it strikes. Easing the mainsheet also helps to relieve the pressure on the sails, and you may need to do both (A) on the following page.

More than once I've been caught out trying to reef an unfamiliar boat in gusty weather. I suggest that you practice reefing with a light or moderate breeze before you need to. Take the opportunity to learn how your boat handles when reefed down—both with and without the jib.

Resume course after the gust has passed

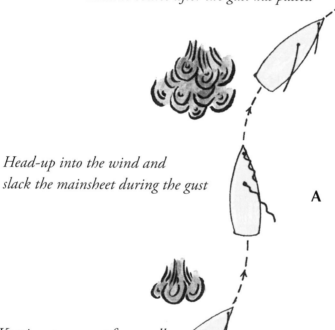

*Head-up into the wind and
slack the mainsheet during the gust*

A

Keeping an eye out for squalls

Heaving-to

There is one other heavy-weather tactic that you should know about. Try pulling the jib over so the wind is blowing on the wrong side, leave the mainsheet about half out, and push the tiller over to leeward—the same side as the boom (B). Most boats will lie to very comfortably, making little or no forward progress but drifting slowly to leeward. This is a useful trick when sailing alone. It gives you a pause to bail, consult the chart, make repairs, or have lunch. It is called heaving-to, and boats in this state are said to be hove-to.

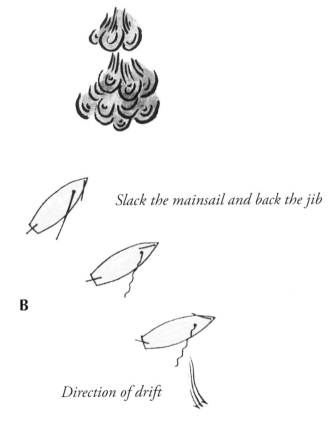

Slack the mainsail and back the jib

B

Direction of drift

Getting under way from a mooring

Picking up a mooring under sail

Chapter 3: Arrivals and Departures

Landing on Docks and Beaches, Picking Up Moorings, Dropping Anchors, and All That

Sooner or later you will have to bring your boat in to a dock, pick up a mooring, or sail off a beach. Keep in mind that you have oars (or should have) and so always have the option of dropping the sails and rowing in or out of a crowded dock, harbor, or marina. It may be less dashing, but it's far, far better to be safe than sorry. There are few quicker ways to make bad friends than by running into someone else's boat.

Letting Go and Picking Up Moorings

This is a lot easier (and less nerve-wracking) than sailing in or out of a crowded dock. Unless there is a strong current, your boat will already be pointing into the wind. All you need do is ship (install) the rudder, lower the centerboard, raise both sails, and slip (let go) the mooring.

Picking Up a Mooring Under Sail

This is a more difficult maneuver because you must stop the boat, or you will run right over the buoy and maybe pull your arm out of its socket trying to hold on to it.

There are two ways to stop a sailboat... three, if you include running aground. Dropping the sails is one. The other is to round up into the wind so the wind itself acts as the braking force.

You can put your boat into the equivalent of low gear by dropping the mainsail and leaving the jib up. In this scenario there is no need to round up into the wind. Sail down onto the mooring, then drop the jib when it's within reach. An alternative is to raise just enough of the mainsail to give you steerage. This has the delightful name of scandalizing the mainsail.

Round-up into the wind, drop the mainsail and then sail down onto the mooring, droppin the jib when it is within reach

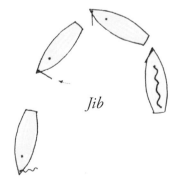

Jib

Mooring

29

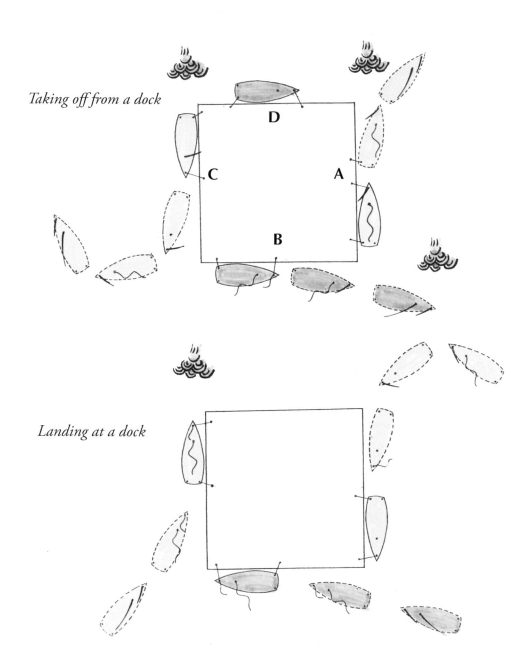

Taking off from a dock

Landing at a dock

If there is any current, always approach the mooring against the current, not with it. If the wind is strong, drop the sails upwind of the mooring, then sail down to it using the windage of mast and rigging to give steerage. This is a useful trick, and is called sailing under bare poles.

Getting Under Way from a Dock

As you already know, backing the jib is pulling the jib over with one of the jibsheets, so the wind is blowing on the "wrong" side. The head of the boat will swing as shown at right. It's a handy way to rotate the bow of the boat, and particularly useful when the boat is caught in irons.

Wind

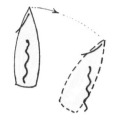

Backing the jib

You can usually hoist a jib regardless of wind direction, but a mainsail is much easier to raise when the wind is from ahead. With the wind blowing from behind, or even from the side, the peak (and often the battens, too) gets jammed in the rigging as you hoist the sail.

Every situation is different, and on the opposite page are some diagrams showing the most common maneuvers when landing or taking off from a dock.

A. Wind Ahead
Lower the centerboard and raise both sails. Then backwind the jib and let go the bow line. The head of the boat, the bow, will swing away from the dock as shown. As the mainsail fills, let the stern line go, bring the jib over, and you are on your way.

B. Beam Wind (from the Side)
Hoist both sails, leaving the mainsheet loose. Let go both mooring lines, haul in on the jib, and then haul the main.

C. Wind Astern
Hoist the jib, let go both mooring lines, then, when clear of the dock, turn into the wind and raise the mainsail.

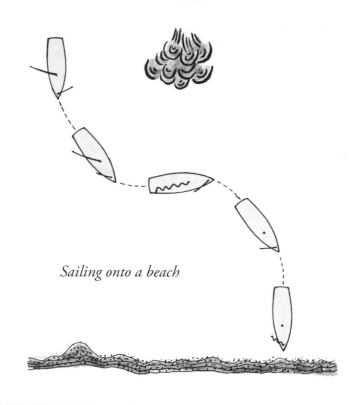

Sailing onto a beach

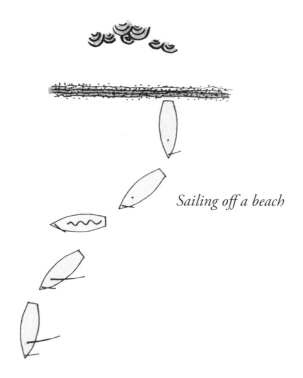

Sailing off a beach

D. Onshore Breeze

When your boat is tied up at a dock with an onshore breeze (wind blowing toward the dock), it can be awkward to get clear under sail. If possible, shift the boat around so it is on the side of the dock, pointing into the wind. Then you are in the same situation as (A) on the previous page.

If shifting the boat is not an option, you could row out, drop an anchor, then hoist the sails, or tie up to a convenient boat or mooring. If you can't row the boat, try tossing the anchor off the dock as far as possible, then haul yourself out until clear and raise the sails.

Another way (better not try this if there's a lot of traffic) is to drop an anchor on your way in to the dock. Tie the end of the anchor line to the boat until ready to leave, then haul yourself out and set sail.

Sailing On and Off Beaches

Wind Blowing Off the Beach

Sailing onto a beach with the wind behind you is easy: even if you do nothing, you are bound to end up on the beach—along with all the other debris. When the wind is blowing off the beach, sailing onto it is much trickier. You will be tacking in shallow water, with little or no centerboard, and may have to remove the rudder as well. Rowing or poling the boat is one option; the other is stepping overboard and towing it inshore by its painter.

Offshore Breeze

With an offshore breeze, it is easy, too easy, to sail off a beach. You just hoist the jib, steer with an oar until you have water enough for the rudder, then head into the wind and raise the main.

I say "too easy" because it's difficult to gauge the strength of an offshore breeze from the land. You may find an alarming increase as you leave the shelter of the shore. I once sailed my International 14 off such a shore and was unwise enough to set the spinnaker. The boat did a somersault, capsizing head over heels, and the mast got stuck in the mud, which made recovery difficult.

Your best bet under these conditions is to take a good look at what the other boats are doing—and not doing. Are they reefed or still carrying full sail? Are they heeled at a crazy angle or only moderately so?

If you are in any doubt, run off under the jib alone until you are far enough from the shore to judge the wind's true force and direction before hoisting the main.

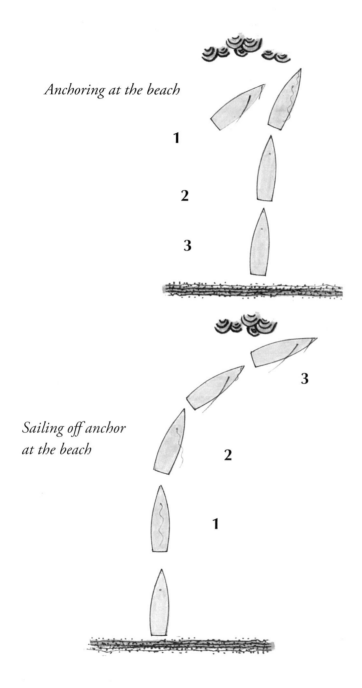

Anchoring at the beach

1

2

3

*Sailing off anchor
at the beach*

2

3

1

Wind Blowing Onto the Beach

When the wind is blowing onto the beach, the strategy is quite different. You are on a lee shore, and need both centerboard and rudder to sail off. If the water is too shallow to do that, about your only option is to row out to deeper water, get a tow, or wade out yourself. If there is a convenient anchored boat or mooring, tie up to it before raising sail.

Dropping an anchor on your way in to the beach will make getting off a great deal easier as shown in the adjacent sketches.

> (1) Come up into the wind when about three or four boat lengths from the shore and lower the sails.

> (2) Drop the anchor and let the boat fall back until the anchor has a good bite.

> (3) After raising the centerboard, pay out the anchor line until the stern is close enough to the shore to step out over the transom.

When leaving the shore, reverse the process:

> (1) Haul the boat out on the anchor line until the water is deep enough to lower the centerboard, then raise the mainsail but don't sheet it in.

> (2) Break out the anchor, and when the anchor line is straight up and down, bear away on a close reach.

> (3) Bring the anchor aboard, stow it and raise the jib.

This trick is particularly useful when there is light to moderate surf on the beach, because it prevents the boat from broaching-to (being turned sideways to the waves) and possibly rolled over.

If you have to remove the rudder in shallow water, then steer with an oar until it's deep enough. If you don't want to run up the beach all standing (with all the sails up), come into the wind, drop the main, and head for the beach under jib alone. You may have to unship (remove) the rudder and steer with an oar when the water gets too shallow.

Tricky Situations

On the next page you'll find examples of tricky situations that you will encounter sooner or later. For each, I've given one possible solution, but see if you can think of others—there is usually more than one.

A You have a boat on either side of you, and the wind and current are in opposite directions. How best to get under way?

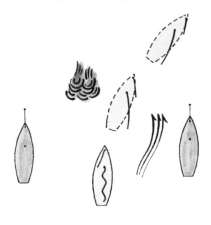

C You are approaching a floating dock, but the only space available is straight downwind. The breeze is moderate and there is no current. What is your best plan? How would you leave the dock under the same conditions?

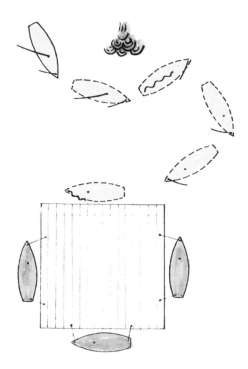

B Same situation as (A), but with the wind and current in the same direction. How to proceed?

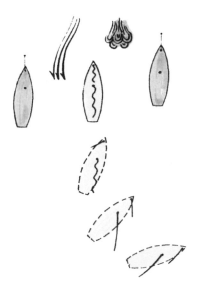

D You are coming alongside another boat at anchor in order to transfer a crew member. There is a strong southerly current and a light breeze out of the west. What is the best way to proceed?

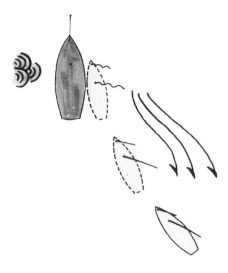

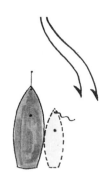

F Same situation as in (D). This time both the wind and the current are strong and in opposite directions. How to proceed?

E Same situation as in (D). There is no current, so the boat is pointing directly into strong, gusty wind straight out of the north. What are the options?

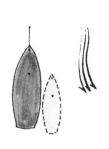

G Same as (F), but the wind and current are in the same direction. What is the safest way to come alongside the other boat?

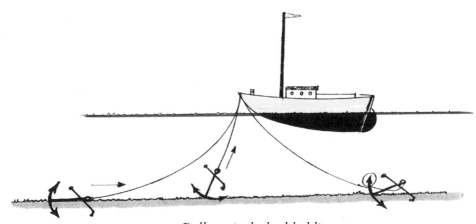

Pull horizontal—good holding

Pull vertical—bad holding

Anchor fouled with line wrapped around a fluke

Anchor rode should be not less than three times the depth of water

Chapter 4: Securing Boats

Making Boats Fast to Fixed and Floating Docks,

Moorings, Anchors, Piers and Other Craft

When you get to where you are going in a car, you just turn off the engine and set the brake. With a sailboat you turn off the power by dropping the sails, but then you must find a mooring, tie up to a dock, drop an anchor, or beach the boat.

Anchoring

Let's take anchoring first. There is quite a variety of styles of anchor available: the traditional fisherman's anchor, the CQR (short for "sec-ure"), mud anchors, and various patent folding anchors.

Anchors hold best when the pull is horizontal, not up-and-down. A length of galvanized iron chain attached to the anchor helps to make this so. The anchor rode (length of line) should not be less than three times the depth of water. Here are some common types of anchor with their good and bad points.

Fisherman's Anchor

Fisherman's

The traditional fisherman's anchor has been around for centuries and is still widely used. Modern anchors are formed of galvanized iron and have folding stocks so they don't take up much room. Such anchors hold well in sand, gravel, and hard mud; not so well in soft mud; and not at all on rock. Be sure to insert the cotter pin, or it may fold of its own accord and lose all holding power.

A drawback to the fisherman's anchor is that a boat is quite likely, with a change of wind or tide, to wrap its anchor line around the upper fluke. When this happens, the anchor is said to be fouled and has little or no holding power. Boats have also been known to sit on their anchors as the tide falls, with unpleasant results.

Danforth Anchors

Danforth

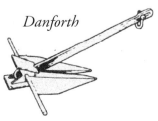

The Danforth is a modern style of anchor, widely used in small craft. It holds better than the fisherman's and has no upper fluke to cause trouble.

Typical mooring

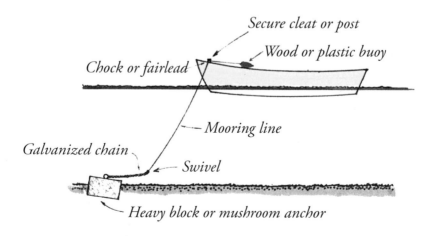

Secure cleat or post

Wood or plastic buoy

Chock or fairlead

Mooring line

Galvanized chain

Swivel

Heavy block or mushroom anchor

Grapnels

Another traditional type is the grapnel. It's like a fisherman's anchor but doesn't fold, and has four hook-shaped flukes. Grapnels are cheap and often used for anchoring fishing nets. They hold pretty well on any bottom except rock.

Grapnel

Mud or Mushroom Anchor

These are excellent in soft mud, but to be effective a mud anchor needs to be heavy. Since it does not fold, it can be a leg-bruising nuisance in a small boat and more useful at the business end of a mooring.

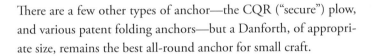

Mushroom

There are a few other types of anchor—the CQR ("secure") plow, and various patent folding anchors—but a Danforth, of appropriate size, remains the best all-round anchor for small craft.

Occasionally, an anchor will get stuck. It may have hooked another anchor, a cable, chain, old tire, or be wedged in rocks. If you can't get it free, tie a float to the anchor line, cast off, and try again at low tide. If that doesn't work, persuade a scuba-diving friend to go down for it.

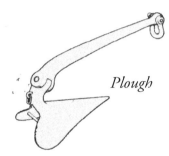

Plough

Using Docks and Moorings

Along with anchoring, there are several other ways to "park" boats: tying them to a floating dock, for example, a mooring, or alongside another boat-(preferably with the owner's permission). Be sure to use fenders (rubber or plastic bumpers) so the two boats can't scrape against each other.

A mooring consists a floating buoy, wood or plastic, attached to a permanent anchor, concrete block, or chunk of granite. Small craft are better off on a mooring than a dock. They can't bang around and jostle their neighbors but just swing with the wind and current, rising and falling with the tide. The disadvantage, of course, is that you still have to get ashore.

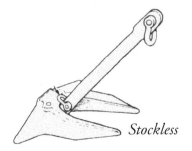

Stockless

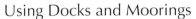

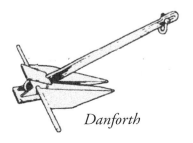

Danforth

Typical Running Mooring, or Outhaul

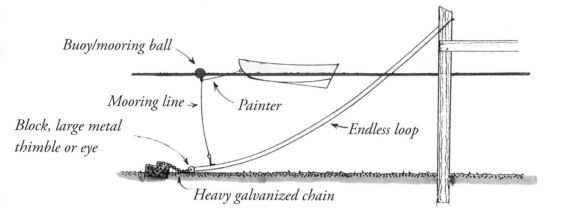

Buoy/mooring ball

Mooring line →

← Painter

Block, large metal
thimble or eye

← Endless loop

Heavy galvanized chain

Typical for Tidal Docking

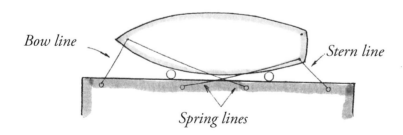

Bow line

Stern line

Spring lines

An ingenious way around this drawback is to use a running mooring (or outhaul). This is simply an underwater block or large eye, attached to a mud anchor or concrete block. After landing at the dock, fasten the boat to the mooring line (which is an endless loop), then haul it out far enough so it can't ground out at low tide.

Docks, Floating and Fixed

A fixed dock, also called a wharf, pier, jetty, or stage head, is a platform, usually with ladders, built out over the water but attached to the shore. You tie your boat up and, like a patient horse, it is supposed to wait until you return.

However, unless you're on some tideless body of water, lake, reservoir, or the Mediterranean Sea, the tide rises and falls—and your boat with it. If you tie it up tight at high tide, you are likely to find it dangling from its painter when the tide goes out.

Much worse is when you tie up at low tide, the water rises, your boat can't rise with it, so fills with water and swamps. Give the boat too much slack, and it will bang around and make a nuisance of itself. So consider not only the wind but the state of the tide when tying up a boat. The diagram shows a common way to do this using spring lines to prevent the boat surging backward and forward.

Some docks, instead of being fixed, are floating so the dock goes up and down with the tide and your boat with it. This is a great convenience, but such docks need a hinged ramp that moves with the dock and can, at low water, be dangerously steep.

In Irons

When caught "in irons" back the jib and push the tiller to starboard

The boat will begin to go backwards swinging clockwise as it does so

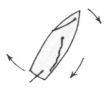

Keep the jib backed and the tiller hard over

Pull the jib over, straighten the tiller and you are off on a port reach

If you want to get off on the opposite tack, back the jib to starboard with tiller to port

Chapter 5: When Things Go Wrong

Running Aground, Capsizing, Broken Gear,

and Other Misadventures; Safety Afloat

Accidents have a way of happening when least expected. Here are some of the things that are likely to happen and how you can cope with them... and be prepared for them.

Running Aground

This is no great matter in a little boat, and you can usually get off by raising the daggerboard (or centerboard) partway and maybe removing the rudder as well. Sailing with neither rudder nor centerboard is awkward, so it's best to drop the sail and row to deeper water. With small boats you can always get out and push. I once stepped on the bottom half of a broken beer bottle, so avoid walking around barefoot. If the mud is really soft, lay down a couple of floorboards or a pair of oars to give you some footing.

Getting Caught "in Irons"

A boat is said to be in irons when pointing directly into the wind, going nowhere with all the sails shaking. Unless quickly corrected, a boat in irons will begin to drift backward and you'll find the action of the rudder reversed. Decide which tack you want to get off on, then back the jib on that side and push the tiller hard over to the other. The boat will begin to pivot as shown on the opposite page. When far enough around, bring the jib over, haul in the mainsail, and straighten the tiller.

Losing a Rudder

Rudders are easily damaged, especially if they project down below the keel. If you do lose your rudder, try steering with an oar just to get you home. Some boats have a cutout in the transom for just such a purpose. Even without this sculling notch, as it is called, you can still steer with an oar over the side—just as you would a canoe.

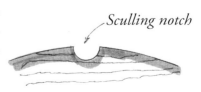

Sculling notch

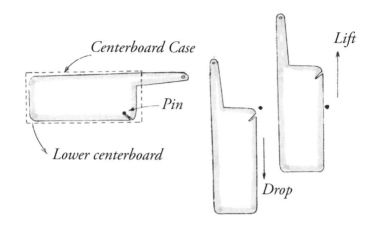

Centerboard Case

Pin

Lower centerboard

Lift

Drop

Righting a capsized sailboat

Jammed Centerboard

It sometimes happens that a centerboard jams and won't go up or down. The likely cause is loose stones, seaweed, or debris trapped in the centerboard case. Metal centerboards usually have a slot for the pivot pin rather than a drilled hole. You can remove one by lowering it and then pulling it straight up through the case as shown. If that doesn't work set the boat ashore and roll it over until you can get at the centerboard.

Capsizing

If you tip an open sailboat too far, it will swamp and fill with water, if the boat has gone over. Modern boats have built-in flotation, of course, you float too, because you have a life jacket on—or should have. But you'll need to get the water quickly out of the swamped boat, and if it has capsized completely, get yourself back into the boat.

The first step is to let go the halyards, pull the sails down, and get the boat upright. If the centerboard is still down, try standing on it, using it as a lever to right the boat. Don't let the oars and loose gear drift away.

If there is not too much wind and conditions are calm, you can often get the water out with a bailer or pump. If water keeps coming up through the centerboard case, stuff a T-shirt or whatever into the slot. When the boat is about half-empty, you can probably wriggle in over the transom (not the side) and finish bailing from inside.

If you can't right the boat, it's better to hang onto it than swim to shore—unless it's very close. A swimmer in the water is much harder to spot than an overturned boat. If you have told somebody on shore where you are going and when you expect to be back, someone will come looking for you. If not… well, you might have a long wait.

Towing a capsized boat is awkward even in good weather. When conditions are rough, it may prove impossible. So, try to get the boat upright and clear of water.

If conditions are really bad, stow the loose gear in the rescue boat and leave your own boat to be retrieved later. Mark the spot by dropping an anchor with plenty of line for the depth of water you are in.

MOB (Man Overboard)

If you or your crew fall overboard, the best way to re-enter the boat is to climb back over the aft (rear) transom after removing the rudder. The same applies if you rescue someone in the water—help them in over the transom. This is safer than over the side because it's less likely to upset the boat.

Rig Breakage

If one of the stays breaks, or a fitting comes loose, you are likely to lose both mast and sails overboard. Try to get the sails off the mast and into the boat, then the mast, spars, and remains of the rigging. Stow them so you are still able to row, and then get out the oars.

Suppose you are out on an exposed body of water when the accident happens—lake, river, estuary, or whatever—and find yourself drifting toward a lee shore. Leave the sails and spars in the water and make fast (tie up) to them with the anchor line or painter. This will slow the rate of drift and keep the bow pointing into the wind. It will also give time for a rescue boat to arrive or for you to decide on your next move.

Losing a Halyard

It may happen that a halyard is let go accidentally and runs up to the top of the mast, or it breaks and the mainsail comes tumbling down. What next? You can't reach the pulley at the top of the mast without either climbing it or bringing the boat alongside a dock on shore.

What you can do is use the jib halyard to hoist the mainsail. Pull the jib down and stow it, then remove the halyard and clip it onto the peak of the mainsail. Since the jib halyard is shorter than the main halyard, reduce the size of the main by reefing it. This is called a jury rig. It may look a bit odd but will get you home.

Beaching a Boat

You may be too far from home when the accident happens, so must beach the boat and walk. If the boat is too heavy for you to drag above the tide range, remove any loose gear and deposit it in a safe place. Lay out an anchor, bow pointing toward the water and, if feasible, a stern line tied to another anchor, tree, or rock.

A worst-case scenario is when you have been forced to land on a rocky beach with an incoming tide and a strong onshore breeze. If you can't drag the boat above the tide range, one option is to remove the bung (plug) so the boat fills with water as the tide comes in. Put enough ballast (rocks from the beach) inside the boat so it won't pound. This obviously is a last resort but could make the difference between a salvageable boat and a wreck.

Getting Lost

I myself have been lost a few times and it can be a scary experience, especially at night or in thick fog. If someone knows where to look, you will be found, but only if you have told someone on shore where you are going and when you expect to return. You will be glad to have the emergency supplies listed on the next page—especially the flashlight and whistle.

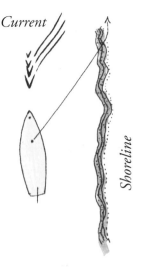

Current

Shoreline

Becalmed

This is not exactly an emergency, but running out of wind could get you in trouble. Dropping the sails and getting out the oars is an obvious first move. But suppose you get caught in a strong current sweeping you downriver and out to sea? Dropping an anchor (if you have enough line) and waiting for the tide to turn is one option. Another option is to row close inshore where the current is less, or even moving in your favor. A fourth choice is to set your crew ashore and have her/him tow the boat with a long line. Leave the centerboard partway down and stay in the boat to steer.

Leaks and Leaking

Some boats may leak a bit (or hold rainwater), so you should always have an adequate bailer or pump along with you. Beware of the cheap plastic pumps that have no strainer to keep out seaweed and muck. They soon choke up and cannot easily be dismantled to clear. So be sure to have a low-tech alternative, a bailer, as backup.

Losing the halyard

Safety on the Water

Here are a few tips on safety

• Modern life jackets or vests (also called PFDs, for "personal floatation device") are a great improvement over the clunky, cork-filled versions of an earlier era, but donning one when you are already in the water is a struggle. As the U.S. Coast Guard says with rare wit: "Don't put it off—put it on". So, don't bring a life vest along for the ride, but wear it, properly adjusted and fastened. Also, life jackets are not cushions, so don't sit on them or use them as fenders.

• Take a good look over the boat to make sure that you have all the gear you should have, that it is in working order, and is stowed out of the way but handy so you can get at it.

• Bring proper clothing and raingear. It can be much cooler on the water than on land.

• Check the weather report and be especially alert for squalls, thunderstorms, and fog. Bring a tide table with you—or at least know the times of high and low water.

• Tell someone on shore where you are going and when you expect to be back.

What You Should Have with You

I have an island home in Nova Scotia, and the family maintains a variety of boats—sailing, rowing, and motor. The water is cold, the open sea is just around the point, and fog can descend with no warning and last for days. Over the years we've compiled a list of the gear and emergency supplies that our boats should carry at all times.

This a minimum, and you may well want to bring additional items such as a cell phone or other means to communicate. Even when sailing on protected water, such as a lake or reservoir, you should still carry some emergency supplies.

• Anchor and Line. You should carry an anchor, preferably a Danforth, weighing at least 15 pounds, and a minimum of 10 fathoms (60 feet) of anchor line.

• One life jacket for each member of the crew.

• Oars and oarlocks. Stow within easy reach a sturdy pair of oars, the right length for the boat, and oarlocks. These should be secured with line or light chain so they won't be lost overboard. I like the Davis pattern (designed for life boats) which cannot be lost.

• A bailer. The larger sizes of plastic jugs used for milk, bleach, and detergent make good bailers. Tie the bailer to the boat with light line, or attach a float so it can't sink.

• Charts, a watch, and a flashlight are all useful.

Emergency Supplies in a Watertight Box
• All-purpose tool or multi-tool. This should include a knife, pliers, and screwdrivers for slotted, Phillips, and square-drive screws.
• A few feet of lacing or quarter-inch line.
• Mosquito repellent and sun block.

- A magnetic compass.

- A bottle of fresh drinking water.

- Flares, including at least one parachute flare.

- The loudest whistle you can buy.

- Matches in a waterproof container.

- A signaling device. Even a small mirror can attract attention from far away—provided the sun is out.

Safety at Night

Sailing at night is an altogether different experience. The familiar landmarks, islands, houses, cliffs, and daymarks are of little or no use. From seaward the shore may be a jumble of flashing colored lights, neon signs, traffic signals, and cars, and it can be difficult to spot navigation markers amid such confusion.

Nor are vessels easily seen from the shore. In the second world war, German U-boats are known to have surfaced off Manhattan so the crew could take snapshots of that famous skyline.

A small boat at night, even with sails up, is practically invisible. It is below the radar, both electronic and human—even assuming a lookout is posted. Avoid, if at all possible, crossing shipping lanes and busy channels at night. Remember that commercial vessels cannot change course or stop suddenly. A container ship or tanker may very well be traveling at 20 knots (25 mph) and takes a lot of stopping. When the wash from a passing ferry knocked me off my Folkboat into the icy waters of San Francisco Bay, it was a good fifteen minutes before the ferry could maneuver alongside to pick me up.

If you are sailing at night and see both a red and a green light and the bearing doesn't change, something is coming straight at you. Make any noise you can—foghorn or whistle—and shine a flashlight on your sails, not directly at the oncoming vessel. The helmsman is then much better able to judge your size, speed, and course and act accordingly.

A particular hazard at night is a tug towing a barge on a long warp, usually a steel cable several hundred feet long. You may not even be aware that the two vessels are connected—especially when the towline is partly submerged. Working tugs display a particular configuration of lights on their mast plus the usual navigation lights. So, if you make a practice of sailing at night, be sure you know what the various lights, fixed and flashing, colored and white, are telling you.

Rule 1. A boat that is running free (before the wind) shall keep clear of a boat that is close-hauled (on the wind).

Rule 2. A boat that is close-hauled on the port tack shall keep clear of one close-hauled on the starboard tack.

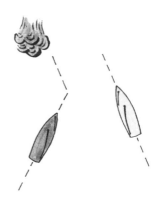

Rule 3. When two boats are running free, but on different jibes, the one that has the wind on the port side (boom to starboard) shall keep clear of the other.

Rule 4. When both boats are reaching with the wind on the same side, the boat that is to windward shall keep clear of the one to leeward.

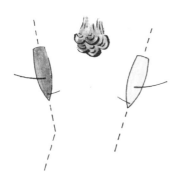

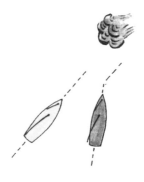

Rule 5. Any boat when overtaking, whether under power, sail or oars, shall keep clear of the overtaken boat.

Chapter 6. Rules of the Maritime Road

Rights-of-Way, Charts, Aids to Navigation, Tides and Fog

Rights-of-Way

Just as there are rules for cars—who gives way to whom at a crossroads, for example—so there are for boats. There are no road signs such as stop, school crossing, or whatever, so it's important that you know the rules and apply them. Don't assume that everybody out on the water knows the rules or intends to follow them. Never forget for a moment that whatever the rights and wrongs of a given situation, avoiding collision is everyone's responsibility.

All the essential right-of-way situations are shown in the diagrams on the opposite page, the boat with the right-of-way being tinted green. In general, motorboats give way to sailboats and sailboats to canoes, kayaks, and swimmers.

Some of the rules may seem unreasonable—a boat running free giving way to a boat close-hauled, for example—but these conventions go back to the days when ships were square-rigged and had very different handling characteristics.

Avoid cutting in front of another boat if at all possible, but pass it astern. Always give other skippers clear notice of your intentions—then stick to them. And don't expect a quarter-mile-long supertanker to get out of your way, because it won't.

This is not a book about sailboat racing (which has its own rules and etiquette), but you'll find a couple of books listed in Chapter 9. It's basic common sense to keep clear of a race in progress, but if you do find yourself in the middle of the wolf pack, don't weave in and out but continue on your course. Ignore remarks about Sunday Sailors or whatever else you might hear.

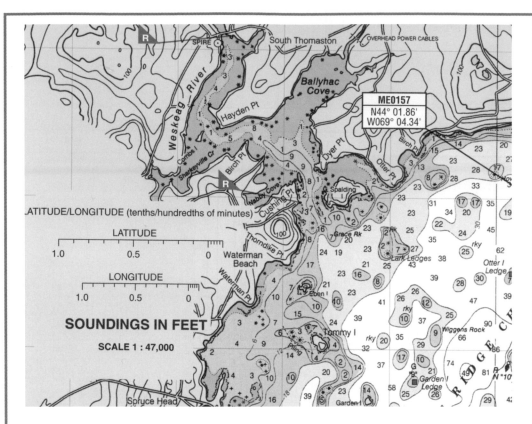

SOUNDINGS IN FEET

SCALE 1 : 47,000

HIGH & LOW WATER
BOSTON, MA
42°21.3'N, 71°03.1'W

Standard Time   Standard Time

DAY OF MONTH	DAY OF WEEK	JANUARY						DAY OF MONTH	DAY OF WEEK	FEBRUARY					
		HIGH				LOW				HIGH				LOW	
		a.m.	Ht.	p.m.	Ht.	a.m.	p.m.			a.m.	Ht.	p.m.	Ht.	a.m.	p.m.
1	T	2 02	9.0	2 10	9.6	8 02	8 29	1	S	2 50	9.8	3 15	9.1	9 09	9 26
2	F	2 42	9.1	2 54	9.3	8 47	9 11	2	M	3 38	9.9	4 09	8.8	10 02	10 17
3	S	3 25	9.2	3 43	9.1	9 37	9 58	3	T	4 31	9.9	5 09	8.5	11 01	11 15
4	S	4 12	9.4	4 37	8.8	10 30	10 48	4	W	5 30	10.0	6 13	8.5	...	12 04
5	M	5 03	9.7	5 35	8.7	11 28	11 44	5	T	6 33	10.2	7 20	8.6	12 17	1 09
6	T	5 58	10.0	6 36	8.7	...	12 28	6	F	7 38	10.6	8 25	9.0	1 21	2 12
7	W	6 56	10.4	7 39	8.8	12 42	1 29	7	S	8 41	11.0	9 25	9.5	2 23	3 11
8	T	7 55	10.8	8 40	9.1	1 41	2 29	8	S	9 40	11.4	10 20	10.0	3 23	4 05
9	F	8 55	11.3	9 40	9.5	2 40	3 27	9	M	10 36	11.6	11 12	10.5	4 18	4 56
10	S	9 52	11.7	10 35	9.9	3 37	4 22	10	T	11 27	11.6	...	...	5 11	5 45
11	S	10 47	11.9	11 29	10.3	4 32	5 14	11	W	12 01	10.8	12 17	11.4	6 02	6 31
12	M	11 41	12.0	...	...	5 26	6 05	12	T	12 46	10.9	1 06	11.0	6 52	7 17
13	T	12 21	10.5	12 34	11.8	6 19	6 55	13	F	1 32	10.7	1 54	10.4	7 41	8 02
14	W	1 11	10.6	1 27	11.3	7 12	7 44	14	S	2 18	10.4	2 44	9.7	8 31	8 48
15	T	2 02	10.5	2 19	10.7	8 05	8 33	15	S	3 05	10.0	3 35	9.0	9 22	9 37

Nautical Charts

Nautical or marine charts are like road maps but tell you where you can go (and not go) on the water instead of the land. Think of them as having a third dimension, downward, showing what you can't see—rocks, a sunken wreck, reefs, and shoals. Charts tell you what you can expect to find on the bottom—sand, shells, mud, or rock. This is useful to know before dropping an anchor, because an anchor's holding power depends to a great extent on the type of bottom.

Aids to Navigation

The International Association of Lighthouse Authorities tried to establish a uniform system of buoyage throughout the maritime world. They failed, so we now have two systems—IALA-A and IALA-B. The first system, IALA-A, is used by Britain, France, most of continental Europe, Australia, and a few other spots. The latter system, IALA-B, is used in North America, South America, plus Japan and Korea. Here is a brief summary, but for the details see Chapter 9 for sources on navigation, buoyage systems, charts, and tide tables.

Cardinal buoys indicate the location of the safest or deepest water.

There are two basic types of navigation markers: Lateral markers show the limits of a channel or waterway, and cardinal markers indicate the location of a wreck, reef, or other hidden hazard. The latter are rather cleverly color-coded so you can tell where the danger lies in relation to the buoy.

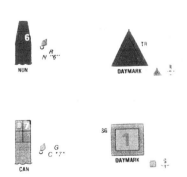

Lateral markers tell you by their shape, color, and numbering system which side of the channel they are on and whether you should leave them to port or starboard when approaching a harbor.

In general, buoys marking the right hand side of the channel are red, conical in shape, even-numbered, and are left to starboard.

PORT SIDE
OR RIGHT DESCENDING BANK
GREEN OR ☐ WHITE LIGHTS (CROSSING)
FLASHING

ISO

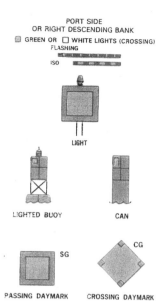

LIGHT

LIGHTED BUOY   CAN

SG

CG

PASSING DAYMARK   CROSSING DAYMARK

STARBOARD SIDE
OR LEFT DESCENDING BANK
RED OR ☐ WHITE LIGHTS (CROSSING)
FLASHING (2)

ISO

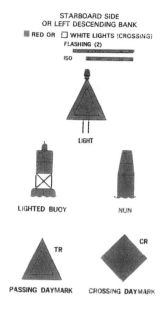

LIGHT

LIGHTED BUOY   NUN

TR

CR

PASSING DAYMARK   CROSSING DAYMARK

PREFERRED CHANNEL
TO STARBOARD
TOPMOST BAND GREEN

Fl (2 + 1) G

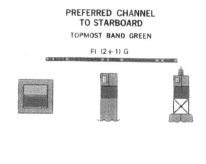

PREFERRED CHANNEL
TO PORT
TOPMOST BAND RED

Fl (2 + 1) R

SAFE WATER
NO NUMBERS—MAY BE LETTERED

RW "N"
Mo (A)

LIGHTED
AND/OR SOUND

A

RW
"A"

MR

G

RW
SP "C"

SPHERICAL

RW "N"

UNLIGHTED
AND/OR SOUND

The left side of the channel is marked with can-shaped buoys, black or green, odd numbered, and should be left to port. Just remember; red, right, returning. However, if by some lucky chance you are approaching an Irish harbor the colors and shapes are reversed (Ireland is part of the IALA-A system). So you might end up red, right... and on the rocks!

This is all pretty straightforward—as long as you know which continent you are cruising—but what about east–west or west–east passages, since you are neither entering nor leaving a harbor? The convention (quite arbitrary, it seems to me) is that the coast is marked as if you were rounding North America in a clockwise direction, from Nova Scotia, say to British Columbia. Cruising from Bar Harbor to Portland, for example, the shoreline (which would be on your right) is marked as if you were entering a harbor—red, right, returning. I know it makes little sense, but that is the accepted convention.

Some buoys have flashing lights so you can see them at night, and others are equipped with various noisemakers so they can be identified in fog. Similar sound sources are as widely spaced along a particular shoreline as feasible. Over a 20 mile stretch of coast you might get a bell buoy, a whistle, a gong, and only then another bell.

Similarly with light patterns: Flashing lights not only conserve their energy source (now usually a solar panel), but are more distinctive—especially when seen against a background of shore lights.

Spar buoys

Small channels, used by local boats, are still often marked with spar buoys, which are now being discontinued by the U.S. Coast Guard. Spar buoys, like other markers, are painted red, green, or black, according to which side of the channel they mark.

Very small channels, the equivalent of footpaths, may be marked by local fishermen on one side (better check which side) with sticks or pieces of brush. Often the stick has an orange glove stuck on top with a pointing thumb, looking a bit like a hitch-hiker.

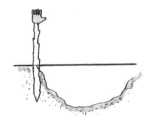

A   B

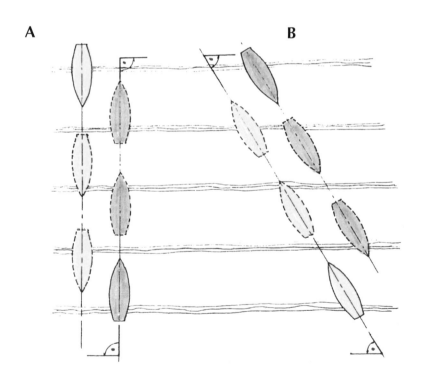

It's astounding how a novice sailor can convince himself (women tend to have more sense) that he is where he thinks he is. I was once sailing a very small boat across Puget Sound to Horseshoe Bay near Vancouver. Certain of my own position, I watched the Vancouver–Nanaimo car ferry entering the wrong channel. "That's odd", I thought, "they must have made a mistake." Needless to say, I had a rude awakening. I tell this story, hoping to convince you not to be seduced by your own cleverness but to carry an up-to-date chart and know how to read it.

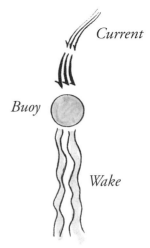

Current

Buoy

Wake

Buoys can also show you the direction and speed of the current. If you get close enough, you can see the wake and make a guess at how fast the water is moving past the buoy. Don't get too close, because buoys, especially in high tidal areas like the Bay of Fundy (25 to 30 feet is common), need a lot of scope. This enables them to veer around in unpredictable ways.

Getting Around in Fog

Nova Scotian fishermen recognize two kinds of fog: thick o' fog and black thick o' fog meaning daytime fog and at night. Black thick o' fog is to be avoided—unless you are very familiar with the shoreline. Better to tie-up and wait for it to clear.

Suppose you are rowing or sailing in thick fog on the open sea or an estuary and have no compass to guide you. The continuous lines of waves, or swells, passing under your boat are a useful reference. Unlike the wind, they change direction slowly, over a period of days. Suppose you are crossing the swells at right angles, as in (A). If you continue crossing them at the same angle, you know that you are going roughly in the same direction and not around in a circle.

Or, say that you are crossing the swells at an angle of 60 degrees (B). If you maintain the same angle, you will continue in roughly the same direction. If you reverse the course, keeping the same 60-degree angle, you will be returning to your starting point. This is a rough-and-ready reckoning and takes no account of tide, current or sideways drift, or leeway.

What Would You Do If...?

1. You are sailing on a broad reach and overtaking a small powerboat. They haven't seen you. Should you yell at them to get out of your way, or what?

2. Your rudder has come off and is floating away, and is already out of reach. What should you do?

3. You are sailing downwind in a narrow channel, and a much smaller boat is beating against the wind toward you. What should you do?

4. You are entering a harbor for the first time and see a bell buoy painted in black-and-white vertical stripes. How close to it can you go?

5. You are sailing on a lake, there are thunderstorms about, and you notice what seems to be a dark patch on the water coming rapidly toward you. What should you do?

6. You are sailing across San Francisco Bay, and you see an odd-looking orange marker floating on the water. You realize it is a racing mark and a dozen boats are sailing directly toward you. What should you do?

7. You are sailing home one evening against an adverse current and the wind is dying. What are your options?

8. You have been offered a tow home by a passing motorboat. Should you lower the sails? Raise the centerboard or leave it down?

9. You are sailing at night and you notice a red and a green light some distance away. They don't seem to be moving, but are getting closer. What does this mean, and what should you do about it?

10. You are sailing across San Francisco Bay on the starboard tack. You find yourself in the middle of a sailboat race with all the contestants on the port tack. What should you do?

11. Your halyard has parted, and the free end runs up to the pulley at the top of the mast. You are a couple of miles from the dock, and the wind is from the side—a reach. What are the options?

12. You have missed the channel and run all standing onto soft mud. The tide has turned and is falling rapidly. What should you do?

13. You sailed off a beach early one morning and when you return in the afternoon, the on-shore wind is much stronger, waves are breaking on the shoreline, and you're not sure what to do. What are the options?

14. You see a motorboat waving. They are out of fuel and want a tow home. There is not much wind. How can you help them?

15. You are out sailing in a strong, gusty breeze when you see a capsized sailboat. One person, with no life jacket, is clinging to the keel. He seems confused and keeps trying to right the boat and wants you to help him. You are pretty sure that the mast is stuck in the mud. There are no other boats in sight. What should you do?

16. You are tacking on a large lake, the water level is lower than usual, and you strike a rock with the daggerboard. It breaks off, and when you pull the stump you find only an inch or two left. The wind is moderate, and home is about a mile away straight upwind. What are the options?

17. You are sailing across a bay when you see very large waves—the wake from a passing supertanker—coming at you. What should you do? Or not do?

18. You want to land on a rocky beach and go ashore for a couple of hours. The tide is falling, and your boat is too heavy to drag without rollers. What is the best way to tie the boat up so it won't go aground before you get back?

19. Your anchor has hooked an underwater mooring chain and you can raise it far enough to see but no further. How can you get clear?

20. You are entering an unfamiliar harbor, under full sail on the port jibe with the wind directly behind. You realize that the channel is too narrow to round up into the wind and drop the anchor as you intended. There are docks to starboard, mudflats to port. What are the options?

21. You are on the starboard tack, and your crew yells that there is a large yacht on port tack very close. Collision is imminent. What should you do?

See pages 86 and 87 for answers

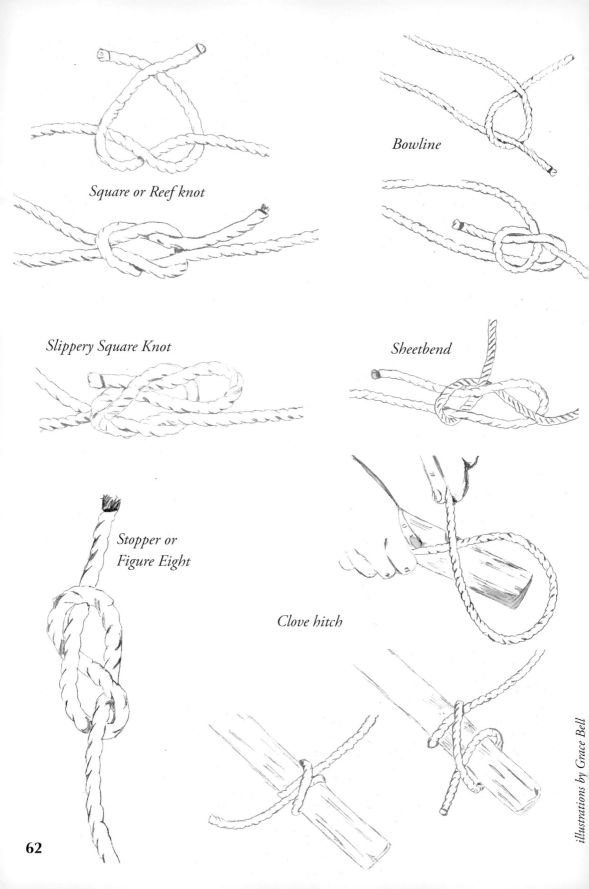

Square or Reef knot

Bowline

Slippery Square Knot

Sheetbend

Stopper or Figure Eight

Clove hitch

illustrations by Grace Bell

62

Chapter 7: Knots, Splices, and Whippings

Several Basic Knots, Two Splices, and Two Whippings

You can get by with two kinds of splices and a few knots—but these you must know well, really well. You should be able to tie (and untie) them in the dark, with frozen fingers and even underwater.

"When is a knot not a knot?" Answer "When it's a granny." A granny may look like a real knot, but it has two flaws: it's unreliable, and it may jam so that you cannot easily undo it.

Basic Sailors' Knots

The Square Knot
Most people already know the square or reef knot because it's used for tying shoelaces and parcels. It is also handy for joining ropes of similar size. If you tuck in one loop, you get a slippery square knot, quickly released by pulling the end—especially useful for tying reefpoints.

The Bowline
This is the knot for making a loop, or noose, at the end of a rope. You can drop it over a piling or make it fast to an eyebolt or anchor.

The Clove Hitch
The clove hitch is another essential knot, especially useful when tying a boat up to a dock. It looks like a pair of spectacles, and you make it by slipping one loop under the other, as shown. You can then drop it over a piling or post.

Figure-of-Eight, or Stopper Knot
This is the standard knot to prevent a line, a sheet for example, from pulling out through a block or fairlead. As with any true knot, it holds well but is easily undone, even when wet.

Round Turn and Two Half-Hitches
This is actually a clove hitch tied around its own standing part. It's a quick way to tie up a boat, a line to an anchor, or whatever.

The Sheetbend
This is the same knot as the bowline but without the loop. It's especially useful when joining two lines of different sizes.

Short splice

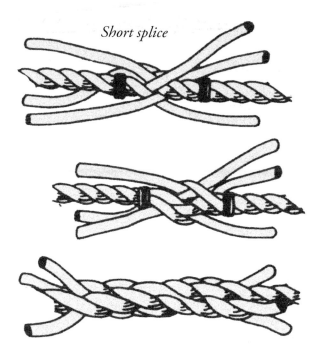

Eyesplice

B

Sewn whipping

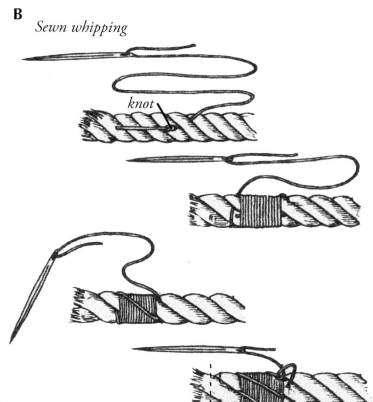

knot

cut line

With galvanized thimble insert

Splicing

A splice is like a permanent knot and was traditionally used for three-stranded rope. The woven or braided type of line requires a different technique which is beyond the scope of this book. (See Chapter 9 for a book on rigging.)

The short splice and the eyesplice are essential, but there are numerous other ways to amuse yourself and practice with old rope; the long splice, the backsplice, the various crown knots, Turk's head, monkey's fist, plus rope fenders and all kinds of mats and fancy work.

Short Splice
The short splice is used to join two ropes of roughly the same diameter end-to-end, using three-stranded rope. It is also a useful way to attach one line to another with no knots or cutting—a buoy to a mooring line, for example. Unlay three or four inches at each end and wrap a piece of tape around the end of each strand to keep the fibers from spreading.

The Eyesplice
This is the handiest of splices with a multitude of uses such as attaching a painter to an eyebolt. Get some old rope, follow the diagram, and practice until you can complete a splice in five minutes (or less).

Whippings

Here are a few ways to whip the ends of three-stranded rope so the strands won't unravel. The fastest/easiest method is to cut ends of plastic line, which are then just melted in a flame (a cigarette lighter works well) or with a hot knife.

(A) This simple whipping requires some thread, preferably waxed, and making windings around the line, tucking the thread under the whippings.

(B) The sewn whipping is more permanent than the first, but you will need a triangular sail needle, a sailmaker's palm or heavy-duty thimble, and waxed thread. Start with a simple overhand/stopper knot. Weave thread back and forth following the lay of the line. Finish with two half-hitches, and pull knot tight, and down between the strands. Be sure to leave some surplus line at the end so you can cut it cleanly with a razor knife when the whipping is done.

A *Simple whipping*

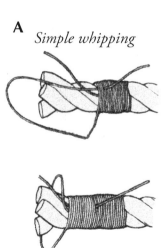

Chapter 8. The Language of the Sea

Words and Phrases Used by Sea Folk, Ancient and Modern

Aback: When the wind is blowing on the wrong side of the sails, it can stop the vessel and even force it to sail backward. You must have heard someone say: "I was really taken aback…."

About: To come about (or go about) is to change tacks so the wind is blowing on the opposite side of the sail. "You're on the wrong tack" used to be a common expression.

Adrift (*or to go adrift*): Out of control and at the mercy of tide, wind, and weather.

Afloat: Opposite of submerged.

Aground: Touching or resting on the bottom. Hard ground means to be stuck with little chance of getting off until the tide turns or help arrives.

All standing: Bringing a boat up abruptly under full sail, either by dropping an anchor or running onto hard ground such as a steeply sloping beach.

Aloft: Above the deck, usually up in the mast or rigging.

Anchor: A heavy hook, usually iron, to prevent boats and ships from drifting. Dropping anchor means what it says, but raising it is called weighing anchor.

Anchor rode: Heavy line or chain attached to the anchor. A useful rule is making the anchor rode three times the depth of water.

Backing (*or backwinding*) **a sail**: Sheeting the sail so the wind blows on the wrong side.

Ballast: Movable weights—rock, iron, or lead—for trimming the boat. Live ballast, of course, is you and your crew.

Battens: Sail battens are thin strips of wood or plastic that slide into pockets in the sail. They help the sail to set and also prevent the leech from flapping.

Beaufort Scale: Invented by a British admiral of that name, the Beaufort Scale is a universal method of describing the strength of the wind by a number. For example, Force 2 is a light breeze, Force 6 a strong breeze, and Force 10 a storm with 30-foot waves and 65–70-mph winds.

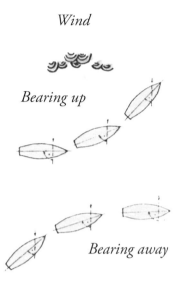

Wind

Bearing up

Bearing away

Bearing away: Changing the boat's direction so as to increase the angle between the centerline of the boat and the wind. If you continue bearing away, you will soon be on a run and eventually have to jibe.

Bearing up: The opposite of bearing away, bearing up is changing the boat's heading so as to reduce the angle between boat and wind. If you continue to bear up, you will find yourself closehauled and eventually have to come about.

Beating to windward: Sailing against the wind by means of a series of tacks.

Blade: The broad, flat part of an oar.

Block: What landlubbers call a pulley. Blocks have a grooved wheel for the rope and are made of metal, wood, plastic, or a combination. Blocks can be single (one wheel) double, triple, or even quadruple.

Boathook: A long pole with a blunt hook at one end. Boathooks are made in wood, aluminum, as well as various composites. They must be buoyant enough to float and be of sufficient diameter so you can get a good grip. Avoid the dangerous variety that telescopes (collapses) when you push with it.

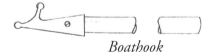

Boathook

Boom: A spar, usually made of wood or aluminum, to which the lower edge, the foot, of the sail is attached.

Bowsprit: A spar that projects out over the bow of a vessel to which a jib or staysail is attached. They used to be called widow makers because men had to go out on them and were often swept away by a sea in heavy weather.

Bowsprit

Breasthook: A triangular-shaped wooden knee that reinforces the bow of a boat.

Broach (*or broaching to*): A sudden, uncontrolled swing into the wind, usually when running before the wind. It can be dangerous and cause the boat to fill and capsize.

Bull's-eye: A small fitting usually made of hardwood such as lignum vitae (ironwood), with a smooth hole for a rope to pass through.

Buoy: A floating marker of wood, plastic or metal, usually anchored to the bottom with rope or chain.

Burgee: Small, pivoting flag at top of mast.

Capsize: When a boat overturns, it is said to capsize.

Cast off: To let go a line or a mooring.

Carvel: A boat built with the planks edge-to-edge is said to be carvel-planked. When the planks overlap a fraction (like clapboards on a house), it is called lapstrake, clinker, or clench-built.

Carvel planking

Centerboard: A swinging metal or wooden plate that can be lowered when sailing against the wind. Without it the boat would tend to slide sideways through the water. Most small-boat centerboards are designed to swing up if you run into shallow water or hit a rock.

Cleat: A wooden or metal fitting to which running lines are attached.

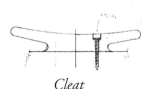

Cleat

Close-hauled: When a vessel is sailing as close to the wind as she is able with all the sails pulled in tight.

Close-reefed: The sails have been reduced by reefing to the smallest possible area.

Cranky: A vessel is said to be crank or cranky when she is unstable and rolls from side to side. It also means an ill-tempered or irritable person.

Daggerboard: A daggerboard is the same idea as a center-board, but instead of swinging, it slides up and down in a daggerboard case. It takes up less room, but when not in place tends to clutter up the boat. Also, if you hit an underwater obstruction with a daggerboard you can do serious damage.

Davis-pattern oarlocks: Designed for lifeboats, Davis oarlocks cannot be lost overboard even if the boat capsizes. If you use square-drive screws, they are not easily stolen—or borrowed.

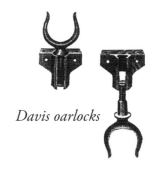

Davis oarlocks

Downhaul: A line for pulling the tack of the sail down so the luff is stretched tight.

Drift (to go adrift): A situation in which a boat is controlled only by the forces of wind, tide, and current.

Draw: A boat is said to draw 2 feet when it needs that amount of water to float.

Eyebolt: A bar of iron, bronze, or stainless steel with an eye at one end and machined for a nut at the other. A screw eye is the same idea but is made to be threaded into wood.

Fathom: A seaman's measure of length or depth. It is still used, and is the distance from fingertip to fingertip, with arms outstretched. It equals 6 feet.

Fairlead: A metal fitting through which runs a mooring line or anchor chain. Fairleads are usually screwed to the rail or gunwale of a boat.

Fairlead

Fairway: A wide, well-marked channel used by vessels.

Fall-off: To increase the angle between the centerline of the boat and the wind. Similar in meaning to bearing away.

Fenders: Rope, plastic, or rubber bumpers hung over the sides of a boat to protect the hull when lying alongside a dock or other vessel.

Fetch: The distance to the nearest shore when measured upwind. It could be a few hundred yards, a mile, or a thousand miles. The longer the fetch, the larger the swells that a steady wind will generate. A rather dubious formula claims: $H = \sqrt{F}$, where H is the height of the waves in feet and F the fetch in miles. So, for example, a fetch of 4 miles could produce 2-foot waves; a fetch of 1,600 miles 40-foot waves.

Flotsam and jetsam: Flotsam is floating debris, and jetsam is what has been thrown off a vessel. Jetsam tends to become flotsam.

Flukes: The heart-shaped blades of an anchor. Also the tail of a whale.

Foot: The bottom edge of a sail, usually attached to a boom with lacing.

Forestay: Forestays run from the bow (or bowsprit) and help support the mast. They may have a foresail attached with bronze clips or hanks.

Foul: An anchor is said to be fouled when tangled with another anchor, chain, or underwater obstruction. The opposite is clear. Also refers to a vessel's bottom when covered with marine growth.

Founder: To fill with water and sink. Usually said of large vessels rather than dinghies, which are supposed to have enough flotation to both stay afloat and support a crew.

Gaff rig: A four-sided sail with a gaff above and boom below. Also called leg-o'-mutton sail.

Gaff rig

Gaff: A wooden spar to which the upper edge of a gaff sail is attached.

Garboards

Garboard: The first plank either side of the keel.

Gooseneck: A swiveling fitting used to attach the end of the boom to the mast.

Goose-winged (*also Wing-and-wing*): A fanciful term for running directly before the wind with the jib on one side of the boat and the mainsail on the opposite. With a strong, following wind, some boats tend to roll alarmingly under such conditions.

Goose-winged or Wing-on-wing

Grapnel: A lightweight anchor, usually with four flukes, for anchoring fishing nets and small craft.

Grommet: A hole in a sail into which a brass or stainless-steel ring is inserted.

Gudgeons: A pair of fittings, screwed onto the transom, into which the rudder pintles drop, for attaching the rudder.

Gunwale: Pronounced "gunnel", the upper, outboard edge of a small boat.

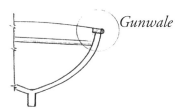

Gunwale

Halyards: Lines, rope or wire, that raise and lower sails. A gaff sail has two halyards—one for the throat, the other for the peak.

Heave-to (*also lie-to or lay-to*): Stopping the forward motion of a vessel by trimming the sails so they oppose each other. Usually a jib or foresail will be hauled aback so the wind is blowing on the wrong side and the mainsheet slacked.

Helm: The steering mechanism of a boat—usually a wheel on a large boat, and a tiller on a small boat.

Hoist: To raise, as in hoist a flag.

Irish pennant: An impolite name for the end of a rope which has unraveled.

Irons: A boat is said to be in irons when pointing directly into the wind, with sails shaking, unable to steer. (Iron shackles were used to prevent slaves and convicts from escaping.) Unless quickly corrected, a boat in irons will begin to drift backward.

Ironbound: A forbidding, inaccessible coastline with no harbors, inlets, or beaches.

Jibe: When the wind catches the wrong side of the sail and it swings suddenly from one side of the boat to the other. This may happen because the wind has shifted or the boat changed course. If the crew is caught unprepared, jibes can do serious damage.

Jury-rig: A makeshift arrangement when a mast or other spar breaks and a temporary repair is made.

Knee: An L-shaped piece of wood, usually with the line of grain matching the shape. Knees are used to reinforce connections between structural parts of a boat—keel to transom, for example.

Knee

Lacing: Light line, cotton or nylon, used to attach a sail to a mast, boom, gaff, or other spar.

Lapstrake: A style of planking (also called clinker or clencher) where the planks overlap, like clapboards on a house or slates on a roof. It was used by the Vikings because the carvel tradition of planking was unknown in Scandinavia at that time.

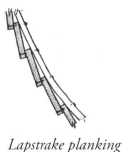

Lapstrake planking

Leeboards: Drop keels hung on each side of a vessel. They were often used on shallow-draft sailing barges, especially in Holland and the Thames Estuary. They have two advantages over centerboards: They don't weaken the hull, nor do they clutter up the cargo space within.

Leech: The after, trailing edge, of a sail.

Leeward: The lee side is the sheltered side of a vessel (or a shore) opposite to the direction in which the wind is blowing.

Leeway: With the wind blowing from the side, boats inevitably drift sideways or make leeway. Keels, centerboards, daggerboards, and leeboards are all designed to slow this sideways motion, but they can't prevent it.

Lee helm: The dangerous tendency of a boat to run off the wind (bear away) when you let go the tiller. (See weather helm.) It's dangerous because it can lead to a jibe.

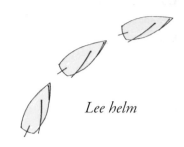

Lee helm

Lee shore: A shore—beach, rocks, or mudflats—onto which the wind is blowing.

Line: Ropes are usually called lines on boats up to a diameter of an inch or so. Heavier lines might be called warps, cables, or hawsers. Never call them strings, or you will be branded a landlubber forever after.

List: When a vessel leans to the right, it is said to have a starboard list.

Loom: The section of the oar between the grip and the blade.

Luff: To luff up is to bring the boat up into the wind, slowing the forward motion. If you continue to luff up, you will end up in irons.

Make fast: To tie up; make fast to a mooring, dock, or pier.

Marconi rig: (also called Bermudan): The most common shape for sails—an elongated vertical triangle.

Mast: A vertical spar for supporting sails. May be supported by stays, but small boats often have unstayed masts.

Missing stays: When trying to come about, the boat may not come around but fall back on the same tack. You may try again—if you have sea room enough—or wear the vessel by turning the other way and jibing (see Wear).

Mooring: A line with a float tied to one end and an anchor or block of concrete at the other. A convenient way to tie up boats so they can swing freely with wind and current.

Oarlocks: Metal or plastic supports for the oars. Also called rowlocks.

Offing: The distance from the vessel to the nearest shore. Of crucial interest to the engineless and unhandy vessels of the past.

Outhaul: A line that pulls the sail out toward the end of the boom and so puts tension in the foot of the sail.

Painter: A short length of rope permanently attached to the bow of a boat. Used for tying-up or for towing.

Pier: A dock where boats tie-up to unload goods or passengers.

Peak: The upper corner of the sail, to which the halyard is attached.

Pintles: Fittings attached to the rudder that drop into the gudgeons.

Port: The left side of a vessel when facing forward (toward the bow).

Reach: To have the wind on the beam, or from the side. A safe, easy point of sailing, sometimes called a soldier's wind. (Perhaps because even a soldier could sail a boat under such conditions?)

Rake: Angle of mast—forward or backward.

Ready about: The usual phrase to warn the crew to prepare to go about. Often followed by "helm's hard a-lee" or "a-lee" when you actually go about.

Reef: To reduce sail area either by tying part of the sail down with reefpoints or by rolling it around a boom or forestay. Also a sharp ledge or underwater outcropping of rock. "When on a reef I came to grief...."

Rigging: Standing rigging is fixed, usually supporting a mast or other spar. Running rigging runs through blocks or bull's-eyes and controls the sails.

Rigging screw: Also called a turnbuckle, a rigging screw is a threaded device with either left- or right-hand threads for tightening wire stays.

Rode: See Anchor rode.

Rowlocks: Metal or plastic supports for the oars. Also called oarlocks.

Rudder: The rudder is hung on hinges at the aft end of a boat and used for steering.

Running: When the wind is from behind and you have both main and jib out as far as they will go, you are running before the wind.

Scope: The extra margin of chain that a buoy or a vessel needs so it is not strained by current, wind, or the rise and fall of the tide.

Sculling notch: A half circle cut out of the upper edge of the transom for steering with an oar or sculling.

Sculling: A convenient way to propel a boat forward with one oar over the transom. Especially useful in crowded harbors.

Scuppers: The drains on either side of a deck. To be scuppered means to be finished, done for, down the drain.

Scuttle: If you deliberately sink a vessel, you are said to scuttle her.

Shackle: A U-shaped link with a threaded pin allowing two lengths of chain or an anchor and chain to be connected. The pins, especially stainless steel, have been known to work loose. Safety a shackle by running a piece of soft stainless steel wire through the hole and wrapping it around the shackle.

Sheer, Sheerline: The top edge of a boat when looked at from the side. Boats can have a lot of sheer, little or no sheer, and reverse sheer.

Sheerlines

Sheets: These are the lines that control the sails. When the sheets are pulled in tight, you are said to be close-hauled. When they are half out, you are reaching, and when all the way out, you are running before the wind.

Shrouds (*also main stays*): The lines, on both sides of the boat, usually wire, that hold up the mainmast.

Soldier's Wind: See Reach.

Spars: Long wood or metal poles to which the sails are attached.

Spinnaker: A large, parachute-shaped sail used only when running before a light or moderate following breeze.

Splicing: To join rope by weaving one part into the other. A short splice and a long splice are used to join the two ends of a rope. An eyesplice forms a loop or noose.

Spring Lines: Crossed lines used when tying up to a dock. They prevent a boat surging backward and forward.

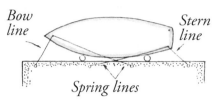

Spring lines

To stand in: Approach the coast.

To stand off: To keep well clear of the land and out to sea. Ever hear someone being called stand-offish?

Standing rigging: A general term for the lines on a boat that are fixed, whether of wire or rope; for example, a forestay or a shroud.

Starboard: The right-hand side of the vessel when facing forward. The word comes from the Norse steerboard (rudder) which was always on the right. The opposite of starboard used to be called larboard, but after who knows how many collisions and near misses, was eventually changed to port. If someone yells "Starboard" at you, they are claiming the right-of-way. Don't argue, give them the right-of-way.

Stays: Stays support the mast and are usually wire because rope has too much stretch. See Forestay.

Steep-to: A seaman's term for a coastline that drops abruptly into the sea with no beach or shelf. This is a poor place to drop an anchor, because you might need hundreds of fathoms of anchor rode to reach bottom.

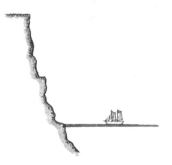

Steep-to

Steerage: To have steerage means you have enough forward motion through the water to be able to steer. You can't steer a boat (or a car) when it is stationary.

Stem: From a Norse word stam, the stem is forward part of a boat, usually curved.

Stops or ties: Strips of canvas used for tying down sails.

Swells: Lines of long waves that don't break until they reach shoal water. Swells can travel thousands of miles across open ocean and change direction only slowly, over a period of days.

Swamp: When an open boat fills with water (usually because it has heeled over too far), it is said to be swamped. You must have heard someone say "I'm just swamped with work".

Tack: To change direction so the wind fills the opposite side of the sails. This is another term for coming about, and is similar in meaning.

Telltales: Short lengths of colored yarn or wool, tied to the shrouds on either side. Telltales show the wind direction, relative to the boat, at that point.

Tides: Tides ebb and flow. An incoming tide is called a flood tide, and an outgoing one an ebb tide. An in between state is known as slack water.

Tiller: A tiller fits into or over the top of the rudder so you can steer. This can be pretty strenuous in rough weather, so vessels of any size are steered with a wheel.

Trim: Describes how the boats sits in the water. Trim can be changed by moving ballast around—or the crew.

Unship: To remove, as in unship the oars, or rudder.

Vector: A line representing a force. Vectors have both direction and magnitude.

Wake or wash: The waves created by a passing vessel. The wake from a large ship can be a serious hazard to small craft.

Water, water: Suppose you are racing and have a boat pinned between you and the shore. If they are in danger of running aground, they can shout "Water, Water," and you must give them room to come about.

Wear: To wear a boat is the opposite of coming about (see Wearing). The boat is steered so the wind is brought around the back of the sail, not the front. At some point you are bound to jibe.

Weatherly: A seaman's term for a vessel that sails well to windward when closehauled. More generally, it means seaworthy.

Weather helm: Most boats have a tendency to come up into the wind when sailing close-hauled. Some weather helm is desirable because if you let go of the tiller, the boat will head up into the wind and stop. The opposite, lee helm, is very undesirable because the boat will run off the wind and eventually jibe.

Weather vane: A pivoting metal flag, usually triangular, that indicates the direction of the wind relative to the boat. It does not indicate the true wind direction unless the boat is anchored.

Windward: The side from which the wind is blowing.

Wearing: This boat tries to come about, fails, and falls back on the same tack. Instead of trying again, the skipper decides to wear. He ends up on the opposite tack as originally intended. Failing to come about is called missing stays. If you do miss stays, you can usually coax the boat into coming about by backing the jib, shoving with an oar, or both.

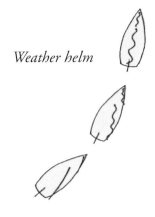

Weather helm

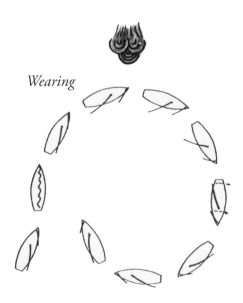

Wearing

Chapter 9. Sources

Books, Magazine, Chart, Tide Tables, and More

Further Reading

Good Reads for Young People...

Swallows and Amazons series, by Arthur Ransome. Published by David Godine.
    Series of twelve books, classic stories of a sailing family in the English Lake District.

Captains Courageous, by Rudyard Kipling. Published by Echo Library.
    An epic tale of fishing on the Grand Banks.

The Night I Flunked My Field Trip, by H. Winkler and L. Oliver. Published by Penguin Books.
    Frank Zipzer leads a nautical class outing awry.

The Star Glass: The Return of Kalifax and Captain Jenny, by Duncan Thornton and Yves Noblet.
    Published by Coteau Books. A Voyage to the Vaastlands in search of vanished Elves.

Sailing Stories and Poems, by The Antique Collectors' Club.
    An imaginative anthology of sailing adventure.

Bloody Jack: The Strange Adventures of a Ship's Boy, by Louis Meyer. Published by Penguin Books.
    Story of a 13-year-old orphan disguised as a boy.

Sailing to the Sea, by Mary-Claire Helldorfer. Published by Penguin Books.
    A young boy spends three days cruising with his family.

Aloha Salty, by Gloria Rand. Published by Henry Holt & Co.
    An eventful Alaska-to-Hawaii cruise in a small sailboat.

The Wanderer, by Sharon Creech & David Diaz. Published by Harper Collins.
    Crossing the Atlantic under sail, told by a 13-year-old girl.

Stanley, Flat Again, by Jeff Brown. Published by Harper Collins.
    Slim Stanley wins a sailboat race and has other adventures.

Workboats, by Jan Adkins. Published by WoodenBoat Books.
    A tale of the sea without varnish and polished brass.

The Sailor's Alphabet, by Michael McCurdy. Published by Houghton Mifflin.
Illustrated nautical terminology for children.

Moominpappa at Sea, by Tove Jansson. Published by Farrar, Straus and Giroux.
A family finds adventure living in an island lighthouse.

Skeleton Crew, by Allan Ahlberg. Published by Puffin Books.
Three skeletons tangle with pirates on a sailing holiday.

Moonsailors, by Buckley Smith. Published by WoodenBoat Books.
Sky-high sailing adventure told through fanciful drawings.

...and for the Rest of Us

The Riddle of the Sands, by Erskine Childers. Published by Penguin Books.
"A thrilling story of spies, sailing and German ambitions before the first World War."
The author later became involved in Irish politics, ran guns for the nationalists, (and
was finally executed by the Irish government) for carrying a handgun.

The Venturesome Voyages of Captain Voss, by J. C. Voss. Published by Gray's Pub.
A scarcely believable account of a round-the-world trip in an Indian dugout canoe
rigged as a schooner. Voss was a magnificent seaman, barely 5 foot tall.

Sailing Alone Around the World, by Joshua Slocum. Published by Sheridan House.
Slocum's entertaining account of his circumnavigation of the globe more than a hun
dred years ago. When Slocum was introduced to President Kruger, of South Africa, as
"the man who is sailing 'round the world," Kruger is supposed to have retorted, 'Not
round the world, across it." The president was a flat-earther!

The Oxford Companion to Ships and the Sea, edited by Peter Kemp. Published by Oxford Univer-
sity Press. A mine of fascinating and mostly useful information.

The Rover and *Mirror of the Sea*, by Joseph Conrad. Published by Wilside Press, and BiblioLife.
Two of Joseph Conrad's best tales.

The Far Side of the World, by Patrick O'Brian. Published by WW Norton.
This is just one of twenty or more well-researched exploits of the Royal Navy during
the Napoleonic era.

Sailing with Mr. Belloc (out of print), by Desmond McCarthy. Originally published by Grafton.

The Strange Last Voyage of Donald Crowhurst, by Tomalin & Hall. Published by International Marine.
> A sympathetic but factual account of a lone round-the-world racer whose abandoned multihull was found in the South Atlantic and brought back on the deck of a British freighter.

The Last Grain Race, by Eric Newby. Published by Lonely Planet.
> The best account published of the last of the great steel sailing freighters. Newby at his best.

Escape to the Sea, by Fred Rebell. Published by Youth Book Club.
> An account of a 6,000-mile trip in an open boat across the Pacific. Rebell improvised everything he needed for the voyage—including his passport.

Adrift—A Personal Saga, by Tristram Jones. Published by Sheridan House.
> Plus several other books on his near-incredible adventures.

Ice Bird, by David Lewis. Published by Sheridan House.
> A chilling account of small-boat sailing in the Antarctic.

South: The Endurance Expedition, by Ernest Shackleton. Published by Penguin Books.
> Describes the 1,600 mile voyage in a 20 foot open boat (the James Caird) after the expedition's vessel was caught in the ice pack and crushed.

Boat Handling and Navigation

Chapman's Piloting, Seamanship and Small Boat Handling. Published by Hearst.
> The standard, indispensable reference book. Try to get a recent edition, as conventions do change.

The Racing Rules of Sailing, by Paul Elvstrom. Published by The US Sailing Association.
> Updated every four years, this is the definitive book on racing sailboats in North America.

Building Small Sailing Craft

Building Classic Small Craft, by John Gardner. Published by Mystic Seaport Museum.

Building the Norwegian Pram, by Simon Watts. Published by Lee Valley & Veritas.
> A building manual and large-scale, detailed plans for building an 11-1/2-foot Norwegian sailing pram. This is too small for adults, but ideal for the younger crowd.

Building Small Boats, by Greg Rössel. Published by WoodenBoat Books.
> Traditional carvel and lapstrake construction for boats under 25 feet.

Clinker Plywood Boatbuilding Manual, by Iain Oughtred. Published by WoodenBoat Books.
Glued lapstrake (clinker) plywood construction, by one of the leading small boat designers.

How to Build the Catspaw Dinghy, by Editors, WoodenBoat. Published by WoodenBoat Books.
A boat for oar and sail, the 12'8" carvel planked Catspaw, designed by Joel White, built with the help of Simon Watts.

How to Build Glued-Lapstrake Wooden Boats, by John Brooks and Ruth Ann Hill. Published by WoodenBoat Books. Exceptionally detailed how-to.

How to Build the Shellback Dinghy, by Eric Dow. Published by WoodenBoat Books.
A fairly simple 11'2" glue-lap-ply dinghy by Joel White, which rows, tows, and sails beautifully.

Knots and Rigging

All the Knots You Need, by R. S. Lee. Published by Lee Valley.

Knots, Bends, and Hitches for Mariners, by US Power Squadrons. Published by International Marine.

The Marlinspike Sailor, by Hervery Garrett Smith. Published by International Marine.

The Essential Knot Book, by Colin Jarman. Published by International Marine.

The Rigger's Handbook, by Brion Toss. Published by International Marine.

Sailors' Knots & Splices, DVD, by Brion Toss, produced by WoodenBoat Videos.

Wind and Weather Forecasting

The Sailors' Weather Guide, by Jeff Markell. Published by Sheridan House.
A comprehensive look at weather for sailors.

Weather to Sail, by Mike Brettle. Published by Crowood.
The complete guide to sailing weather.

Eric Sloane's Weather Book, by Eric Sloane. Dover Publications.
Explains weather in a relatively simple, and humorous manner.

Boating/Sailing Magazines and Books

Magazines
        British publication *Water Craft*: www.watercraft.co.uk
        American publication *WoodenBoat*: www.woodenboat.com
Books
        Lots more books at:
        www.woodenboatstore.com
        www.boatingbookstore.com
        Many out-of-print titles can be ordered from www.abebooks.com

Nautical Charts and Tide Tables

Charts produced by NOAA, NIMA, and the British Admiralty are all available from
        www.nauticalcharts.com, an online catalog.

You can print out a tide table, present and future, for any location in North America by going to www.tidesandcurrents.noaa.gov

1. As the overtaking boat, you have the obligation to keep clear. This applies to any overtaking boat, whether powered by oars, sail, or motor.

2. Use an oar as a makeshift rudder or row over and retrieve the rudder.

3. The boat that is running free has to give way. This is an old rule dating back to the days when most vessels were square-rigged and could alter course without risking a jibe.

4. This is a middle-ground marker, and you can go as close as you wish.

5. This is likely to be a squall, so get the sails down as quick as you can and try to keep the boat's head up into the wind.

6. Get clear of the mark if at all possible. If not, continue sailing in the same direction until clear of the race.

7. The two options are to row the boat, or tow it from the shore. An adverse current is usually weaker close to the bank because it is out of the main stream.

8. Always drop the sails when under tow, because it is better for the sails and reduces drag. Raising the centerboard also reduces drag, and so does keeping to one side of the propeller slip stream of the towing boat. If the boat veers around at the end of the tow rope, you may need to steer. Sometimes just ballasting the boat with weight in the stern makes it tow more comfortably.

9. Another boat, sail or power, is coming straight at you. If your boat doesn't carry lights, shine a flashlight on your sails. This is preferable to pointing the beam directly at the oncoming boat because it shows your course, speed, and situation more clearly.

10. Carry on sailing in a straight line until clear of the race.

11. If you can't climb the mast or hook the loose end with a boathook, drop the jib and hoist the reefed mainsail with the jib halyard.

12. Drop the sails, dump any movable ballast, rocks, sand, water, etc. overboard, and shove with an oar. If that doesn't work, get out and push, supporting some of your weight on the boat. If necessary, take up the floorboards to get a firmer footing, or stand on a pair of oars laid flat on the mud underwater.

13. Your best bet is to drop the sails and row the boat, stern-first, through the surf. As soon as you touch, jump out and pull the boat up the beach. Avoid getting turned broadside to the waves, because you are likely to get rolled over—which could easily break the mast and damage you!

14. Have them drop an anchor with plenty of line, then take one of the crew ashore to fetch fuel. An alternative is to lend them your oars and rowlocks—if they fit.

15. Try getting the person into your boat over the stern. If that is impossible, give him a life jacket and help him into it. Keep a line on him so he can't drift away, then try to get help from shore or any craft within signaling distance. Don't hesitate to use one of your flares to attract attention.

16. Rowing home is the obvious course. However, you may be able to improvise a leeboard using one oar. Lash it in a near-vertical position on the lee side of the boat and try tacking. Even a floorboard can serve as a leeboard in an emergency.

17. It's always best to meet waves head-on. If they come at you sideways, they could swamp the boat or roll it over.

18. One way is to drop an anchor on your way in, about three boat-lengths from the shore. Make the bow of the boat fast to the anchor line, then scramble out with a stern line and tie it to a tree, rock, or a second anchor. Never mind if you get wet in the process—your boat will be safe until you return.

19. Pull the anchor line in as far as possible and make it fast. Then pass another line—painter, or whatever—underneath the chain, pull it tight, then make it fast. Lower your anchor and see if it will come loose. Let go the temporary line passing under the chain, and you are free and clear.

20. Your only option is to round up into the wind and put your boat on the mudflats. This may cause some merriment on shore, but we all have moments of ignominy.

21. It's most likely that the crew of the yacht has not seen you. If you have a foghorn handy, sound it. Don't wait for the other boat to respond, but go about immediately and steer clear.